CLIFTON SANDS

To Mark

With great appreciation,

All the Best

Alex Dyall

For Maria, Sam and Aaron

CLIFTON SANDS

Alex Boyall

Copyright © 2024 by Alex Boyall

All rights reserved.

The right of Alex Boyall to be identified as the author of this work has been asserted in accordance with sections 77 and 78 of the Copyright, Designs and Patents Act, 1988.

No part of this book may be reproduced or transmitted in any form or by any means without prior permission in writing from the publisher.

The story, all names, characters, and incidents portrayed in this production are fictitious. No identification with actual persons (living or deceased), places, buildings and products is intended or should be inferred.

Front cover painted by Screwdriver artist, Johno Cornish Check out more of his excellent work at Johnocornish.com

CHAPTER ONE

Hi, I'm Dalian McIntyre. Irish yes, just like it's owner, and a bit of a mouthful I know, so it's Mac to most. You might have heard of me, I'm the guitarist in the band Rebel Shout. Our single made it into the charts, 'She's on it'.

Maybe you bought it?

No, I thought not.

It's not that we were shite, we were actually pretty good. I was on lead guitar, Jase was our front man on vocals and bass, then Lance played drums. We were an all new, hard edged power pop trio, young, hungry for stardom and ready to take on the world.

It had all started so well. I remember Alice, my then girlfriend, rushing up to me after a gig in Camden Town bursting to tell me that an A&R man wanted to speak to us. He introduced himself as Ritchie Bartez, a fast talking American formerly based in LA before being headhunted (or so he claimed) by Lazor Records here in the UK. He was looking for the next big thing to take over the music scene. He took us to Soho, to a Vietnamese restaurant that none of us had ever heard of, to talk business. We ordered a multitude of oriental dishes and drank champagne, it really was a pinch me moment.

"You guys rocked tonight, seriously. The crowd loved you. I'll tell you what I'm gonna do, I'm gonna set up a showcase for you guys so my bosses can come check you out." His white veneers glistened at us. "What do you say?"

"Sure, yeah, definitely!" Jase jumped at his proposition, looking at each of us as we all nodded in enthusiastic agreement.

"Alright, cool. You guys would do great in LA, they love English rock bands over there. Have you ever been?" We hadn't.

"I'll get you there one day, I promise," he winked.

"What bands have you worked with in LA?" I asked as I gulped another mouthful of champagne.

"Are you kidding me? Have you heard of The Strokes? Sum 41?"

"Wow! Yes, of course I've heard of them!" I couldn't hide my excitement.

"Well a whole bunch of bands just like 'em, that's who. Who wants another drink?"

Jase, Lance and I exchanged glances, our faces glowed at just what was happening to us. We continued to indulge ourselves, Ritchie stood up.

"Listen, I'm gonna take off you guys. Here's my card, don't lose it. I want you to call me at my office tomorrow and we'll get this thing started up. It was terrific seeing you guys tonight, I've got a good feeling about this, really I do. Enjoy the rest of the evening, it's on me. I'll talk to you tomorrow." He winked again, flashed his pearl smile and glided out.

For the rest of the evening we discussed what had just happened. We weren't naïve enough to completely celebrate as in reality he was just some American we had met at a gig. We couldn't be sure if he was the real deal or just some bullshit blagging Yankee? Either way, he had just paid a four hundred pound restaurant bill.

As it turned out Ritchie was true to his word, for the most part anyway. We were thrown into a whirlwind blur of showcases, record company executives, plush record company offices, music industry lawyers and contracts. Before we knew it we had a two album record deal and artist management representation. Holy shit, we'd landed. The record company wanted us in the studio straight away and they knew exactly what song they wanted us to lay down. In what seemed like an instant, our first single was recorded, finished and released upon the unsuspecting youth.

Yeah, well, it did okay. It made it into Radio 1's top 100 playlist and scraped into the top 40 downloads at number 39 before disappearing from both in a few short weeks. So it didn't exactly set the world on fire but not to worry, I mean come on, it was our first single. We returned to the studio filled with hope, momentum and fire in our bellies. We put everything we had into the next recording, this was going to be the one. We proudly presented it to the record company and, well, that's when shit started to go sour.

They didn't like it. They were disappointed. They delayed the release and we were passed from person to person for a while before they admitted that they had decided they did not want to release it at all. We went back to the writing room and started to draft other songs we thought they would be happier with. Weeks passed without a word. Then an email arrived stating they had decided to terminate our contract. They expressed their deepest sympathy and told us to never give up, but just that they were giving up with us. Of course we were straight on the phone to Ritchie. Ritchie would sort this, right? We were his discovery, his baby, this reflected badly on him, surely? He wouldn't be about to stand by and let his next best thing be cast aside without demanding his bosses give us one more shot, right?

Only Ritchie didn't return our calls. His secretary seemed very well versed in the phrase 'Mr Bartez is not available right now, if you'd like to leave another message?'

It was just like that, the dream was over. Pretty much anyway, it didn't take long for disappointment to turn to disillusion, and for despondency to turn into disharmony. Soon fingers were being pointed, blame was being attached and the three of us as a unit simply imploded.

Rebel Shout were done.

It was all very tough to take, I won't lie to you. I'd learnt a very hard lesson, we all had. The thing is, when you spend most of your youth, as I had, playing in struggling, wannabe bands, people don't realise how much hard work it really is. The time, effort and dedication you put in often goes unseen. When you get onstage and play your set in front of an audience it's all people see and judge you on. They certainly never give a thought to the long hours you spend writing songs, rehearsing, working and reworking your material, honing it and then rehearsing some more. No one gives a thought to all the money you spend on guitars, drum kits, amps, strings, stands and sticks. Oh, and a shit load of leads. Then there's the cost of regular rehearsal rooms and transportation to get to all your gigs. Don't even get me started on the costs of studio time. No wonder rock musicians are all skinny, most of them can't afford to eat half of the time. So, yes sir, it's a long way to the top if you wanna rock n roll, alright.

We thought we'd broken through, that we had been given our big chance, but the truth was we'd only made it to the starting line. Unfortunately, all it took was for us to fall at the first hurdle for our race to be run.

So, yes, it hurt. A lot.

Then there was Alice. She and I had met at a gig in Islington around a year and a half ago. We hadn't been together long as a band but by then we had created a bit of a buzz for ourselves around the London club circuit and could pull in a decent crowd. The crowd were great, everyone was sweaty, enjoying themselves. She stood out though. She had long jet black hair that flew around her head as she danced and dark eyes that were locked on me whenever I looked up from my guitar. I was hooked.

Once we had finished the gig I desperately scanned the room. I was standing with Lance when I spotted her. She was leaning up against a pillar, minus her two friends, clutching a half full bottle of Vodka Ice, her eyes already on me.

Lance glanced at me and followed my gaze.

"Save a bit for me," he leered.

"No chance," I ran over to her.

We hit it off immediately, she was funny, if slightly drunk, but I could tell she was smart with it. We talked until the lights in the club signalled for us to go home. She asked me if I wanted to join her for a nightcap back at her place, I could always get a taxi home from there, right? Right. Only I never rang for a taxi because I never left, in fact within three weeks I'd moved my stuff in.

She lived alone in a flat above a launderette on Tottenham Court Road and was able to afford it as she had a good job working in a bank. It was certainly a step up from the dingy basement bedsit in Clapham I'd been staying in. Alice loved the band, to the point where she came to every gig without fail and knew the words to every song, she even sat in on the odd rehearsal when she wasn't working.

I remember the day I gave her the news that we were getting a record deal. She screamed in excitement and threw her arms round me. When she pulled away she was actually crying tears of happiness. I guess she was just so pleased for us. The band being on the brink of success elevated our relationship to the next level. I was totally infatuated with her.

The beginning of the end, it seemed, was giving Alice the news that we'd been dropped by our record label and management. She seemed just as devastated as I was, but I was in a state of mourning. I paced around the flat in self-pity for weeks. Alice became bored of my moping and started going out on her own. When I did venture out, I wasn't the best company. The band rehearsals reminded me of our failure, half of the time Lance wouldn't bother coming and I could tell Jase wasn't that interested anymore.

I found myself more often than not spending the evening alone with just my guitar and red wine for company. Alice started arriving home later and later, not even bothering to let me know where she was. You can probably guess where this is headed. She grew colder and distant towards me. I didn't want to believe what my life was spiralling into.

When Alice didn't come home at all one night, I was forced to confront what was happening. I had tried to call her but she cancelled each time. Somehow I knew she wasn't lying dead in a ditch somewhere. I spent the rest of the night restlessly going over and over the confrontation that would inevitably take place when she returned.

I was awoken by a car door being slammed outside. Dread overwhelmed me as she opened the front door. For a moment we just stood staring at each other from opposite ends of the room. Alice broke the deadlock, let out a sigh and walked over to place her bag down on the coffee table. There was a steeliness in her expression as she returned her gaze to me.

"Look Mac, I'm not going to sugar coat this, things haven't been right between us for a while," she began looking at the floor. "And the truth is, the truth is, I'm not happy with you."

My mouth became dry. "I think you should leave, Mac."

I nodded and looked around the room. I couldn't hide my tears as I began to gather my belongings. I don't know how long it took for me to pack, but the entire affair was in silence.

She watched me place every item into my bag. She did not shed a single tear. As I headed for the doorway, I turned back to her.

"Who are you happy with, Alice?" Her body began to shake.

"You obviously have someone else, I think I deserve to know who it is." She regained composure then looked me up and down.

"Lance," she whispered. I swear she almost smiled as his name left her lips.

Lance.

I felt like I'd been punched in the stomach, I just stood there, the brutality of her honesty rendered me wordlessly dumbstruck. I reached into my jacket pocket, fumbled around to find my key and threw it at her. A fleeting image of me maniacally lunging forward and jamming it into her open eye socket flashed across my mind. Instead, I closed the door and walked away.

CHAPTER TWO

My only option now was to admit defeat and get on the first bus back to my folks' house in the suburbs. It wasn't a long journey but it was certainly a lonely one. My head reeled as I tried to make sense of what had just taken place. I may have become numb from the trauma of the contract termination and subsequent disintegration of my band but I was red raw from the morning revelations of the double betrayal of both my girlfriend and band mate. The images of their faces and Alice's words tormented me.

I got off the bus and walked the short distance up the street to my parent's modest semi-detached two up, two down. I was ten years old when we upped sticks and moved to this house from the family home in South Armagh. My father had a good career working on the trains as an engineer when the opportunity to take an identical position on the London railway had come up, only for much better money. They agreed on the move with the premise of making a better, more prosperous life for us all in a big city.

My folks though, rather naively, had neglected to factor in the cost of living rise that comes with moving to a capital city from a small town, thus we ended up really no better off. Nonetheless, my parents decided to stay, and settled quite happily over the coming years in the English city of London.

Now, as I stood in front of the privet hedge, immaculately manicured by my father, I lifted the latch of the black metal gate and walked heavy heartedly towards the front door. My mother welcomed her failure of a son back home with support and sympathy. I found it both humbling and embarrassing. As I sat in the family kitchen and relayed my sorry story, my father mostly listened in silence, occasionally nodding and making 'hmmm' sounds. My father was the quiet type but when he did speak, he didn't mince his words.

"I've a good mind to pay her a visit at that bloody bank she works at tomorrow and give her a piece of my mind!" My mother was evidently not the quiet type. She placed a steaming hot cup of tea and some chocolate cookies down on the table in front of me.

"Thanks Ma, but I'm not sure that would be the best thing right now."

"No, well, the pair of 'em catching syphilis, that'd be the best thing, I'd say." She added.

"Jeez, remind me never to fall out with you, won't you."

"You need to find yourself a nice girl again, like that one you used to see, what was her name? Lucy, yes, Lucy, I liked her."

"She was a shoplifter Ma, she was arrested nine times for it."

"She had a kind heart though that one, and she was always buying you all those nice new clothes and such."

"She wasn't buying them, she was stealing them. Putting me in receipt of stolen goods hardly constitutes an act of kindness now does it?"

"Ah, well, we all have our faults Dalian, to be honest you could do a lot worse."

"I know, from a shoplifter, to a heartless cheater. I'll date a cattle rustler or something next time shall I? For god's sake…"

"Don't be swearing at your mother," my father interjected. "Now then, take your case upstairs, the room is made up, you're fine to stop with us till you get back on your feet."

"Thank you both. I'm going to go unpack my bags and lay down for a bit, I didn't get a lot of sleep last night."

"Oh bless you," she leaned forward and kissed me on the cheek.

Once upstairs I put down my stuff on my childhood single bed and walked to the window. I looked out at my parent's neat back garden as my father emerged from his shed. He picked up his spade and began to dig the earth of his vegetable patch. It was a Saturday, and spending time like this in the garden was his favourite weekend pastime. May had come, and spring was transforming into summer. It was a beautiful day out there. I reached up and pulled the curtains tightly shut, the room became dull and stuffy. I walked back and sat down on the bed next to my case. I laid staring at the dark ceiling going through how I had ended up back here, I began to cry. I think I cried myself to sleep that afternoon.

Jase came round a few days later. His father owned a construction business so he had always been pretty well off. His family lived in an affluent street in West London with plenty of space so we often stored our band equipment there. Jase offered to drop my guitar and amp off at my parents' for me. I'd always got along and worked with him better than I had with Lance. As we sat in my folks' garden now though, the atmosphere was more than a little muted.

"Lance came over yesterday, to get his drums back," He broke the silence.

"Terrific. I guess you're all filled in then?"

"Mate, I'm so sorry. Please believe me, I had no idea this shit was going on between them, I wondered what the hell she was doing there too."

"She was with him? What did she have to say?"

"Nothing, she stayed in the van the whole time." I stared off into the distance, trying not to think of them together. "I was disgusted when he told me, it made me sick, honestly Mac. Then he started saying he's got himself a new gig already, I could see he was foaming at the mouth to tell me all about it but I cut him off. I refused to give him the satisfaction, the smug bastard."

"Oh, well," I sighed. "You know what Jase? Maybe they deserve each other."

"I hope they get what's coming to them."

"Yeah... syphilis my mother says." We both laughed at that one.

"So where to go from here? What are you gonna do next Mac?"

"I dunno mate. Need a bit of time to get myself together, you know?"

"Sure."

"How about you?"

"Well, love life aside, we're kind of in the same boat aren't we? I mean I love the music, but Maddy you know, she wants us to get a place. My Dad has offered me a position in the company," he trailed off, looking down at the floor.

"Hey, I wouldn't blame you, give you both some security,

and Maddy's a great girl." He was silent for a moment.

"Maybe that's all there was, Mac. Maybe that was it. Our fifteen minutes of fame."

"More like fucking ten wasn't it?" We laughed again.

When Jase left, we hugged and wished each other all the very best, and meant it. As I walked back inside and closed the door I had nothing else on my agenda except moping, skulking, generally feeling sorry for myself and doing very little. My parents however, had other ideas.

"Oh by the way I've found you a job," Dad announced. He said this without as much as a glance up from his newspaper.

"A job? Really? Where?"

"Yes, well some paid work for you at least, over at Mally's shoe shop on Bellingham Road."

"Shoe shop?"

"Fred Mally is an old friend of mine, he's the owner, we chatted on the Euston line yesterday and he said he was looking for someone to do a bit of work for him, I said you needed something to get you out of the house. He wants you there at nine tomorrow."

"Oh right, thanks. Did he say what I'd be doing?" I tried to not sound completely disheartened.

"No," he replied, he turned over to the next page of his *Daily Express*.

The next morning on my walk to Bellingham Road I pondered just how important footwear was in terms of fashion and youth culture. To many, what you wore on your feet was more important than anything else you had on. For the cool kids it was all about the trainers, no doubt about it. It started when you were at school, begging your mum for those hundred quid Nikes all your mates seemed to have and their parents all seemed able to afford, but you were stuck with the ten pound on sale Pumas. Humiliating. Even when you grow out of the school social pressures, shoes are still important for how you want to be perceived by others. Maybe I would be doing something worthwhile after all.

My ponderings ceased as I approached Mally's shoe shop. First glance promised me that issues of youth culture weren't to be of any relevance here. From the racks of plain, unbranded shoes on display in front of the two windows, it was clear that this was a discount shoe store, catering for the elderly and those with meagre budgets. The sort of clientele to which fashion and style held about as much relevance as astrophysics.

I turned the handle of the shop door and pushed it open. The ding-a-ling of a tiny bell above it heralded my arrival. A man who was strikingly similar to Bob Hoskins was leaning, arms folded, on the shop counter facing me. He looked up from reading a newspaper as I stepped in.

"Mr Mally?"

"'Allo son, you must be Damien!"

"Dalian," I corrected.

"Oh, not to worry," he said, as if this was somehow a disappointment to him.

"My Dad said you had some work for me?"

"Indeed I do lad, well then, let's get you started. First thing's first, how about a cup of tea?"

"Oh yes, that'd be lovely, thanks."

"Well, me too! Go on then, you can make yourself one an' all, mine's the West Ham mug," he said returning his attention to his reading material.

"Right." I scuttled past him. To my right was a tiny kitchenette with an ancient looking fridge, a counter with a kettle, bread bin and three jars on it marked tea, coffee and sugar. To my left were two further rooms, one was clearly the stock room as the door was open to reveal, unsurprisingly, a multitude of shoe boxes. The other I assumed to be the shitter.

"Milk and two for me, there's a pack of digestives top left cupboard," he shouted back to me. I returned with his hot tea in the West Ham mug and his packet of biscuits. I stood sipping my own tea in the only other mug I could find, a chipped 'Only Fools and Horses' one. The words 'You Plonker, Rodney!' were written below Del Boy's gurning face on the side.

"So what is it you'd like me to help out with?" I asked, hoping to ascend from my current position as tea boy. "I think I'll be great working with the customers and I'm happy to sort the stock…"

"Nah, nah son, your office is out there," he pointed towards the window. I followed his gaze out to the pavement that fronted the shop. Confused, I looked back to see he was lifting four sealed cardboard boxes out from beneath the counter. He pulled an old penknife from a drawer in front of him and cut the seal on the first box.

"There's two thousand in each, here you go," he handed me a stack of fliers.

They read:

> Mally's Shoe Shop Special Deals!!!
> Save £££££££££s!!
>
> •••
>
> Big reductions on Loafers, Brogues,
> Moccasins, Ladies Ankle Boots, Wellingtons!
> Half Price Orthopedic Sandals!
>
> •••
>
> This Week Only!

So this was it, handing out bloody leaflets on the high street, Jesus Christ.

"Gotta drum up some business son, attract some new punters in, ain't exactly been booming lately, but you're 'ere to change all that ain't cha boy?" He grinned, pushing the first of the boxes across the counter towards me. I stared at it. "Oh yeah, course," he said misinterpreting my look, "how does ten quid an hour sound?"

Like daylight robbery, I thought.

"Sure…" I replied.

"Cash in hand of course," he winked. I nodded, took a deep breath, picked the first box up and headed out to the busy street.

Outside, I placed the box in the middle of the pavement, reached down and pulled a first handful of fliers out. I thought about how would best to make this bearable over the coming hours. At least it wasn't pissing it down. I decided first to try the cheery salesman approach. I put on a bright smile and thrust my flier-holding hand out to the first person coming my way, a thick set man in a black bomber jacket and tracksuit bottoms.

"Good morning sir, would you like…"

"Fuck off," he sidestepped me without a glance and marched past.

How charming. "You have a nice day now!" I called after him. It didn't take me long to figure out that most people were no more interested in receiving this flier than I was in giving it out, I honestly couldn't blame them. I changed my approach by simply stating 'Shoe sale' as I passed out the leaflets. My smile was replaced by a look of couldn't give a shit if you take it or not indifference.

By midday my feet were aching and I was gasping for some lunch, maybe a beer to go alongside it. I glanced across the road to see a girl standing in a shop entrance, she appeared to be giving me a serious eyeballing. She was wearing a tight red t-shirt, denim mini skirt and white trainers. Her long, blonde, Pamela Anderson-esque hair tumbled over her elegant shoulders. She was absolutely stunning. I smiled, she smiled back and cocked her head quizzically to one side. Then she stepped forward, looked left and right to check for traffic and began to cross the road towards me.

I began to panic, she was coming over. Play it cool Mac, play it cool.

"I know you don't I?" She began. "You're in that band aren't you, Rebel Shout?"

I could not believe I was finally being recognised! "My sister wouldn't stop playing that song of yours, she bloody loves it, and that picture of you on the cover…" she continued.

"It is you isn't it?' She fluttered her eyelashes.

Then she looked down at the discount shoe shop fliers in my hand. Never had a single look held such momentary significance. She looked back up at me.

"Rebel who? Never heard of them," I said, shook my head and followed up with a horrible fake laugh. "Not me I'm afraid, no, you've got the wrong guy, sorry."

"Oh..." She looked unconvinced. "That's a shame, I was planning on making my sister one very jealous girl indeed." She began to turn away with a wickedly trouser popping smile.

"Oh well, see ya then."

"Yeah. See ya," I mimicked.

Shit... Bollocks...

I watched her walk away, her rear end wiggled seductively in blue denim above her long, tanned legs. Fred Mally appeared beside me, evidently having witnessed this encounter through his shop window.

"I knew it son, I just knew it! Good lookin' boy like you, all you 'ad to do was flash them pearly whites to bring 'em running eh!" He pushed his arm into my side. "Is she comin' back? Which ones was she interested in then?"

"The orthopaedic sandals I think." He smiled. "Mr Mally, I was gonna see if I could break for lunch, is there any chance of a sub?" I asked.

"No worries Damien my boy." I didn't bother to correct him. He pulled out a ten pound note and handed it to me. "I will take it out of today's wages."

"Thanks. I'll be back in an hour."

CHAPTER THREE

My lunch consisted of the world's blandest cheese salad sandwich and a pint of lager. Apart from a smattering of lunchtime drinkers seated at various tables in what was a relatively small pub, I had the actual bar area to myself. An old man, occasionally breaking into violent bouts of coughing, shovelled silver coins into a noisy, migraine-inducing fruit machine at the far end of the bar.

"White wine spritzer please," the next drinker ordered at the side of me. He didn't take any notice of me, nor I of him, that was until he handed over a ten pound note and took his drink. A tattoo on the back of his right hand caught my eye, a dark serpent that appeared from under his shirt sleeve and snaked up to his index finger.

"Where did you get that tattoo? In jail?" I asked, casually.

He froze, the glass an inch from his lips. Slowly and menacingly he lifted his arm back down to replace the glass on the bar and turned his head to face me, a darkening frown creased his brow, I turned to look up at him for the first time. As my eyes met his, he began to mirror my smile.

"Oh my god. Mac, is that you?"

"Hello Ben!" I said with a grin.

"Jesus, long time no see, man, how the devil are you?"

"I'm good thanks mate, it is great to see you." It truly was.

Ben and I had first met back when I was about nineteen, he was a couple of years older than me and the front man in a four piece soft rock band. I'd seen an advert in a guitar shop in Denmark Street for a band playing their own material that were looking to add another guitarist. I was just starting out and hadn't been in a serious band before, so I replied to the ad. This turned out, of course, to be Ben's group.

I went along for an audition a few days later, I had to try not to laugh upon my first meeting with the singer, Ben, dressed as he was in a Hawaiian shirt, skinny black jeans and a paisley bandanna tied around his shoulder length black hair. He was redeemed, however, by his infectious personality, Ben talked really fast and laughed almost constantly, he was the original life and soul of the party. This therefore meant that people, particularly females, naturally gravitated towards him, a handy trait for a singer. Musically though, it didn't fit what I wanted to achieve as a guitarist so I didn't stay in the band for long.

The man standing before me now looked very different from the long haired, wannabe rock star I'd met that day.

"So, I'm guessing either you joined a soul band or you got yourself a real job, eh?" I smiled, looking him up and down.

"Oh this," he patted his suit. "Yeah, well… Jenny got pregnant, wanted to settle down, it was time to shape up and get responsible I guess. Her dad helped me out and got me a job." I hoped it was better than the one mine got me. "I started at the bank three years ago, I'll be pushing for Branch Manager in a couple of years," he forced a smile.

"That's great man, really, I'm pleased for you, so you've got a little Benny junior then?"

"Ha, not quite. Macy is two and a half, a proper Daddy's girl she is though," he beamed.

"Anyway enough about me, I heard you got signed! What is it like living the life of a pop star?"

Ah shit. I relayed the whole sorry story, the rise, the fall, the infidelity, the humiliation. I decided to leave out the most recent part, the one where I was handing out shoe shop leaflets barely an hour ago.

"Oh man, you poor bastard," he laughed.

I laughed along myself, I guess it wasn't so terrible really in the grand scheme of things, nobody had died, had they? As we left the pub to reconvene our vastly different occupations, we exchanged numbers and swore this time to keep in touch. My heart had been warmed and my spirits lifted by this chance meeting with Ben.

I was still feeling a cheery glow as I re-entered Mally's shoe shop.

"Alright son? All fed and watered are we? Now then, bit of a change of plan, Dorothy next door has asked if she can commandeer you for the afternoon, so we agreed she can have you afternoons this week and I'll have you mornings, that alright with you?"

I took a step back to get a look at the shop next door. Above the entrance the sign read Dotty's Sandwich Bar. Ok, so I'll be cleaning tables, maybe some basic food preparation? I could do that.

"There you go son, the sandwich board is right there by the doorway, should fit your shoulders fine, I don't think it's too heavy, all you gotta do is walk up and down the street. Money for old rope innit!" He laughed. I stared at the sandwich board in horror. An old woman, I presumed to be Dotty, appeared in the window of the shop. She smiled widely at me as she pointed at the board and gave me an enthusiastic thumbs up.

Oh dear god, no. No. That was it. Something gave inside me. If this was the straw that broke the camel's back then fine, fuck the camel, I'll put it out of its misery, give me a gun, I'll shoot the thing myself. I raised my hands up either side of my head and placed my fingers against my temples. Christ, I needed to sort my shit out and do better than this.

"I… I can't do this, I'm sorry Mr Mally, I really can't, it… it's… my agoraphobia!" I stammered.

"Your agro what?"

"My agoraphobia, it's come back, I probably should have mentioned it before, oh god, will you look at all this open space? I've got to go, right away, sorry Mr Mally."

I fell out of the shop as they watched me leaving in disbelief. Once around the corner and out of sight I slowed the manic walking pace down to normal and took a few deep breaths. I needed to sort my shit out and do better than this.

I arrived home just as my father was leaving for his afternoon shift. I explained briefly that Mr Mally had only needed me until lunch today and that he'd give me a call when he next wanted me in. He looked a little unconvinced and quite surprised, though not as surprised as he'd no doubt be when he found out about my previously undiagnosed agoraphobia, should he bump into Fred Mally. I would deal with that when it came to it.

I'm not sure how far from rock bottom I was at this point,

but aside from handing out shoe shop leaflets in the street, I'd lied to my father, lied about not being in Rebel Shout and lied about having a serious mental health condition, all in the course of a single day. This wasn't good. Yet, life's a funny thing, for out of the blue I was about to be handed a paddle that might just help me navigate my way out of shit creek.

To my surprise, Ben texted me a few days later.

The message read:

'Alright Mac? How's it going? I take it Green Day haven't come calling? Listen to this, my mate Adam spent last summer in Edmouth, on the south coast? He was playing guitar in this summer season band at The Clifton Sands Holiday Camp, it's a three month gig, wedding band standards, six nights a week with accommodation on the camp thrown in. It's decent money too, he's been all set to start again with them but he's gone and wrapped his bike round a lamppost, got his arm in plaster for the next eight weeks so he's had to blow it out. What do you reckon, fancy taking his place? Would get you out of London, you can get a seaside suntan and there's bound to be loads of holiday totty gagging for a bit of Mac action. What do you say, shall I text you his number?'

He had to be joking, a holiday camp cover band? Me? Seriously, playing bloody ABBA and Shania Twain songs to a bunch of dribbling geriatrics with little kids running riot on the dance floor every night?

No thanks.

I was about to text him these very thoughts when reality hit me. I had no band, no proper job, no prospects and no plan, maybe this wasn't such an absurd proposal after all. It was paid work, playing music and I wouldn't have to worry about bumping into any ex-girlfriends or band members. At the very least I'd be able to save pretty much all my earnings so when the season finished I'd have a decent bit of money to start afresh. I literally had nothing to lose. I texted Ben for Adam's number. He sent it to me, signing off with:

'Never give up on your dreams! Hi De Hi!'

A few days later, I was stood on the platform at Paddington station waiting for the train bound for Edmouth. My phone call to Adam had gone well, he was an affable enough guy and was happy to fill me in on all things Clifton Sands. He said he'd call the entertainment manager and set up an audition for me as well as emailing over the set list so I could choose three or four songs to play with the band when I got there.

After my initial trepidation I was warming to the idea of spending my summer away from London. I could easily play this stuff on autopilot and just take the money every night. My pride was hurt that I was potentially subjecting myself to everything I had once said I hated, but then again, no one in Edmouth knew who the hell I was! Apart from my parents, no one had any idea that I was even going to be here, let alone why. I could pull this off without anyone ever knowing and just pocket the cash. Such were the perks of no one giving a shit about you. Above all, taking this job gave me purpose and meant getting my train wreck of a life back on track, for the foreseeable future at least. My parents had been happy for me when I told them. My mother likened it to falling off a horse and getting straight back on. I couldn't help thinking it was more like falling off a horse and getting back on a seaside donkey, but I kept that to myself.

An hour and a half after boarding the train, a black cab dropped me off in front of a big red sign that read:

CLIFTON SANDS HOLIDAY CAMP

So this was it, not exactly Caesar's Palace but my residency to be, nonetheless. I took a deep breath and stepped through the entrance.

"Good morning, how can I help you?" the receptionist smiled.

"Good morning to you," I smiled back, "my name is Dalian McIntyre, I'm here for my audition with the house band."

"One moment please." She pressed an internal number on her desk phone and waited for a reply. "Graham? It's Chloe at reception, there's a musician here arrived about the band… Okay will do." She put the phone down.

'There'll be someone with you shortly, please take a seat, Dalian."

I sat down on a bright red plastic seat nearby. Outside I could see all the different families making their way towards the exits. They were armoured with buckets and spades, windbreakers and back-breaking picnic bags. Most were pushing pushchairs and herding excited, sun creamed children around them as they headed on, beach bound. The adults were already red and sweaty from the exertion of these efforts in the rising heat of the day. I felt like an alien in this place.

The entrance door burst open and a tall, thin, balding man with glasses and a pointy nose strode towards me, clipboard in hand.

"Hello, hello! You must be Dalian, nice to meet you! I'm Graham Garner, Head of Entertainment here at Clifton Sands," he stuck out his hand. He had an unusually high pitched Yorkshire accent.

"Hi Graham, nice to meet you too," I shook his hand. He took the seat next to me and turned in to face me. Our knees touched awkwardly.

"How was the train down, not too crowded I hope?"

"No, no, I got a seat the whole way, it was fine."

"Good, good, well normally we do only accept musicians from the agency as you may be aware Dalian, however, you were put forward with quite the credentials, I hear you're a pop star?" He gushed.

"Oh, well, hardly." I began.

"So, come on, tell me. Would I have seen you on *Top of the Pops*?"

"Erm… I think that show ended when I was a kid, I'm sure my folks used to watch it though?" I offered.

"What? I don't think so, my wife and I watched it the other night I'm sure, though, come to think of it George Michael was on it so maybe it was, I don't know, a replay?"

I don't know what was more surprising, the revelation that Graham thought *Top of the Pops* was still running or the fact he had a wife. Nonetheless the exchange was a stark reminder of how monumentally different the musical landscape of this world was.

"Any road," Graham continued, "it's lovely you're here, let me tell you what's going to happen. I'll take you down to meet the boys in the band and they'll put you through your paces, so to speak, then I'll come back and show you which cabin you'll be staying in while you're here. Unless of course you fail the audition in which case I hope your train ticket is a return, ha ha! No, no I'm just having a laugh, I'm sure that won't be the case, ha ha, if it is though there is a ticket office at the station if you need it."

"Right, got it," I forced a laugh.

"Alrighty then!" He clapped and jumped up. "Follow me, I'll take you down to the function room."

I followed Graham as he stepped briskly ahead of me out into the bright sunshine and down the floral lined pathway weaving his way through the crowded walkway. His attention momentarily drawn to a young man in gardener's overalls who was busy watering a flower bed of yellow rose bushes.

"Give them roots a good soaking won't you Matthew." The young man nodded in reply, then raised his eyebrows at me.

As we reached the cavernous function room, Graham held the doors open for me. The first thing I noticed was the giant glitter ball on the ceiling. In front of me as the vast room stretched out were a series of large round tables with the chairs neatly stacked on top. These gave way to a dark wooden dance floor area, and at the rear of the room was the stage. A drum kit sat in the middle with a keyboard setup positioned to the left. A back line of PA speakers and a couple of amplifiers lined the rear curtain.

To the right was the bar area and it was here, seated at a table, that the expectant faces of two men peered up at us as Graham took us over. The two men looked oddly similar, both appearing to be in their late thirties, balding and with moustaches. I thought perhaps they might be brothers.

"Can I introduce you to our keyboard maestro Leon, and Wayne here on the drums."

The three of us exchanged smiles and nods.

"Hi, my name's Dalian but everyone calls me Mac, hopefully I'm gonna be your new guitarist!"

"Right, I'll leave you all to get acquainted, come and give me a shout when you're done eh?" Graham strode towards the exit.

"So, did Headmaster Graham give you the line about the ticket office being open if you needed to be on the next train home?" Wayne asked.

"As a matter of a fact he did!" I replied.

"Oh dear, well don't worry about him, he's a bit of an old woman," Leon reassured me.

"Yeah, he says that to all the new kids, I'm sure you'll do fine."

"In fact, from what we've heard," Leon exchanged a look

with Wayne, "you're somewhat overqualified for this gig?"

Before I could answer, however, a flushing noise came from the toilets followed by the sound of a hand dryer.

"Oh and yeah, by the way, you're not the only newbie here today, we had a last minute change of singer too." Wayne nodded in the direction of the lavatories.

"Oh right, taking a shit is he?" I grinned.

My grin was soon wiped from my face when the ladies door began to open. Out stepped a pretty young woman with a strawberry blonde bob.

"Mac, meet Gina."

CHAPTER FOUR

After the four of us sat down and had the standard introductory chat, our audition took place. It's fair to say we all hit it off, which was a good start. Leon and Wayne, it transpired, were founders of this group and had been the nucleus for the last eight years with pretty much a revolving door of singers and guitarists. Outside of the summer season they played the rest of the year doing the pub and club circuit in various local bands. As we chatted it was impossible not to notice Leon's hand resting on Wayne's thigh throughout, which made it obvious they were, in fact, a couple.

The audition itself was an absolute sail through. I won't be flattering myself to say performing these three songs was not a huge artistical challenge for me. Nor was it for my newly acquainted female band mate who sang with an effortless ease and class. With three songs nailed, Leon and Wayne were standing to offer the two of us their congratulations on getting the job, accompanied with a slightly embarrassing round of applause. I was in. Though I remained unsure of just what I'd let myself in for.

"Oh by the way, do we have a name? The band I mean?" I asked.

"We certainly do, congratulations on becoming a season time member of The Starlight Movers!" Jesus wept, I was sorry I asked. The name made me cringe.

"Terrific!" I grinned.

Graham reappeared shortly after to be told that the four of us were now officially a band. He duly produced short contracts for us to sign before escorting Gina to her new lodgings on camp before coming back to do the same for me. As we walked, Graham decided to return the conversation to my recent pop star past.

"So, my wife says she thinks you were in Billy Idol?"

"What? Er, no, er, he had a song called *Rebel Yell*, she's probably thinking of that, I was in a band called Rebel Shout."

"Oh I see, with Billy Idol?"

"No, no, nothing to do with him, he's more of an eighties guy anyway, I think."

"Well that's me lost!" He threw his arms in the air and laughed theatrically.

"How long have you been in charge here, Graham?"

"Oh, too bloody long, let's put it this way, you get less for murder!" He leaned uncomfortably close to me. I could smell the sour peppermint on his breath.

"Does your wife work here too?"

"Only if she has to, cover mostly, if one of the younger lasses is off."

"She's got other interests then?"

"Oh she likes her arts and crafts, makes jewellery out of all these funny coloured beads and stuff, sells 'em at fêtes. Never makes any bloody money mind, not really, more of a hobby I suppose, but it keeps her happy so I let her get on with it, it's her thing, and you know what they say Dalian lad, happy wife, happy life."

We walked further on through the camp past rows of identical, neat white wooden chalets. Families were sitting out front on deck chairs relaxing and enjoying the sunshine while children played various ball games and threw frisbees to one another. All very British, I thought.

Abruptly Graham turned left in front of me down a path towards an area sectioned off with six foot wooden fence panels. We stopped in front of a tall gate marked 'Staff Only'. Graham unlatched it and showed me through. Once inside, the path ended with the closed off area split into two outbuildings to the left and what looked worryingly like a rundown storage shed to the right.

"Here we go then, these two buildings over here are long term storage facilities, both are locked up, nothin' exciting, mostly spare tables and chairs and what have you. This 'ere to your right is your accommodation." He pulled out a large bunch of keys and began fishing for the appropriate one. Not a storage shed then but my digs.

Unlike the pristine white chalets that we had passed in rows, this was far smaller and appeared to have been painted green originally, but clearly had not seen any such coat of paint in years, as all that remained had all but cracked and flaked away. Graham found the key, unlocked the door and pushed it open for me to enter. I peered inside, admittedly with some trepidation. To my surprise the room inside appeared immaculately neat, clean and tidy.

"I got Elena to clean this one, now there's a lass who's worth her weight in gold, works all hours like a bloody trooper and always does her best job. Should be standard practice for any employee shouldn't it? But you try finding one like her, no, she's a diamond in the rough that one. Problem is youngsters nowadays they don't want to work do they? I don't understand it but there it is. They'd sooner be sitting at home under a duvet playing on their bloody XBox or whatever all day. Yep, if I could clone Elena I would alright."

Well, whoever Elena was, the evidence all around this dwelling clearly proved Graham right.

"Sure, it looks plenty fine to me. How come it's on its own tucked away here?"

"There's a few of them dotted about over the site, they were put up when the camp was originally being built as somewhere to stay for a few of the long term contractors, hence why they're so old. The plumbing's all been updated not long back though so it's not like you've got a tin bath out back, or a hole in the ground outside to do your business in." At least I didn't have to shit in a hole outside.

"Pleased to hear that. So where is Gina staying?"

"She's got one like this across the camp, south side, near the launderette."

"Right," I said trying not to sound too disappointed that we weren't going to be immediate neighbours.

I perused my new homely surroundings. To my left was a metal framed, single bed made up in tight white sheets with a beige blanket on top and a single, but plump, matching pillow. At the base of that was a narrow pine wardrobe with a single drawer underneath. Good job I travelled light. To my right was a tiny cooker, microwave, a single kitchen cupboard and a stainless steel sink and drainer. The centre of the room, or the living area if you could call it that, had a round glass coffee table and two small wicker chairs, each with a single cushion, presumably for if I chose to entertain guests, or in this case, a guest, singular.

I walked the short distance to the back of the chalet to a final area hidden behind a thin, sliding door. I pulled it back to reveal a bare minimalist shower cubicle, white sink and toilet. Whoever designed this was clearly expert in the understanding of the word compact.

"There's no TV I'm afraid, but what do you think? Will it do you alright for twelve weeks?"

"Sure, absolutely, it'll do me just fine, thank you," I said and meant it. My home comfort wants were minimal and I rarely watched TV anyway. This place had everything I needed. Sure, everything was old but at least I had my own shower and, as Graham had more or less put it, at least I didn't have to shit in a hole.

"Good. Right you are then, I'll leave you to unpack and get settled," he tossed two door keys onto the bed before turning and leaving. I placed my suitcase onto the bed, unclasped it and began putting my clothes away. I put my toiletries in the bathroom and took out the rest of my possessions, a dab radio and a dog-eared paperback novel. Like I said, I travel light.

That done, I sat on my bed and took stock of my present situation. The audition was done, I had gotten the gig. I now had a regular and reasonably well paid income for the next three months, not long admittedly, but a platform at least with which to take the next step, whatever the hell that was going to be. It was too soon to have any clear picture of the imminent future, it was only my first day in this place after all. I took a deep breath. Above all else I was still working as a performing musician. At least that's what I kept telling myself. Anyone associated with Rebel Shout would be rolling round on the floor laughing at me for this I'm sure. Part of me, wanted to bolt out of the door right now, run back and jump on the first train back to London. Another deep breath. I'd be okay. This wasn't my life now, just three months out of it, that's all. Time to get on with it.

Later that afternoon I joined my new band mates in the function room to begin playing the chosen songs we would be performing routinely for many nights to come. Listen, I'm not going to bore you by reeling off the set list numbers, if you've ever seen a wedding function band of any kind then you know already the sort of music we were playing. The sort of music your Nan would shuffle arthritically around on the dance floor to, whilst children slid across the floor on their knees. Those sort of songs.

During breaks we chatted and generally began getting to know each other, the music itself coming together quite comfortably. Wayne and Leon were old pros, me and Gina the new kids on the block. The guys were easy to talk to and made us feel completely comfortable. As musicians both were highly competent, Wayne was a solid drummer and Leon an adept keyboardist. As people, both were intelligent, dry humoured and amiable. Then, of course, there was Gina. As soon as she had opened her mouth at the audition we all knew she was a cut above. Good singers were always hard to come by anyway but Gina had a terrific voice.

She sang with a sassy, blues tone, almost like Beth Hart does. She had a great figure too, model like. Leon and Wayne were open and friendly from the beginning, however Gina was far less forthcoming, it's not that she was shy at all, she was actually very matter of fact but she definitely seemed guarded somehow. Perhaps she was just one of those people who didn't give much away until they knew you better. This in turn only made me want to get to know her better.

CHAPTER FIVE

When the opening show arrived, I became overwhelmed with the feeling of stage fright. I had never experienced this before in any of the bands I had ever been in. It started about an hour before we were due to first take the stage. I had just changed into the onstage clothes I had been issued with, prison style, and politely, but firmly, told not to deviate from them. Me, Leon and Wayne were now stood in the dressing room each wearing identical pastel blue short-sleeved shirts, dark chino trousers and black brogue shoes. I felt utterly ridiculous. Doubt, once again, began to fill my mind.

To take my mind off things I decided to take a peek round the stage curtain to see if many punters had started arriving. I was shocked to see the massive room was already two thirds full.

"Filling up out there is it?" said Wayne nonchalantly.

"Er, yeah," was all I could muster in response.

"Opening night is always rammed. It's the start of the silly season. Peak holiday time, guess that's why we're here."

I felt anything but casual. The closer we got to going on the more my anxiety levels rose. I felt uncomfortably hot and my face felt flushed. I thought I could do this but now I was suffering a growing crisis of confidence that was threatening to overwhelm me. All this felt so wrong, so bloody alien. I didn't belong here, simple as. The dressing room door opened and Gina walked through. She was wearing a long, black strapless dress that hugged her figure. There were clearly not the same restrictions on her wardrobe attire as we had, but then we were visually, in essence, her backing band. The sight of her was a welcome distraction. She seemed every bit as relaxed as the other two. Gina went over to sit at her dressing table where she began making her last minute hair and make-up adjustments.

"Are you okay Mac? You look sweaty. You're not nervous are you?" She looked over at me.

"Me? Oh god no, it's just a bit hot and stuffy in here isn't it?"

"Ha! Wait till you get out under those stage lights if you want to know what hot is!" Leon laughed.

"Yes, I do remember how hot stage lights can get actually," I answered, trying to keep my voice even. I thought maybe everything might be alright once we finally got on stage.

I thought wrong. Once Gina introduced the band and we launched into the first number I could barely look up from my guitar, crippled by paranoia I thought everyone was staring at me, the misfit guitar man onstage. I started to hit wrong notes as I struggled to focus and maintain concentration. I became aware of occasional worried glances in my direction exchanged between my new band mates. I needed to get my shit together, and quick. If I could just make it to the end of the night.

Then, towards the end of the first set, I noticed someone standing by the front of the stage, someone who genuinely did seem to be staring at me. For a long time I continued to stare down at my fretboard, trying only to get through these songs until I could stand it no longer. I snapped my head up and looked fully into the face of the person in question. It turned out to be the face of a boy of around fifteen or sixteen. I could see he had Down's syndrome and he broke into a huge grin as our eyes finally met. I looked at him and smiled back, offering him a quick thumbs up with my right hand. He immediately responded with a delighted double thumbs my way and another big grin. At least I seemed to be making someone happy. I felt a little of the tension ease inside me. A couple of songs later and Gina announced our first set break. I breathed a sigh of relief as I took off my guitar and placed it onto the stand behind me as the others made their way off stage to the dressing room. A voice called to me from the front of the stage.

"Hello, excuse me." I looked round to see a woman with long blonde hair in her thirties at the front of the stage standing behind the young lad from earlier. She had her hands placed on both his shoulders. Both were looking at me.

"Oh, hello there," I walked over to the edge of the stage.

"This is Robbie," she said looking at him and smiling.

"Hi Robbie!"

"He doesn't say much, he's a bit shy, aren't you love? But he loves music and he thinks you're really good on the guitar."

"Oh, well thank you."

"Would you mind ever so much signing an autograph for him? He's somewhat of a collector, you'd like that wouldn't you Robbie?"

Robbie nodded enthusiastically and held out an old fashioned autograph book up to me. I'd been asked for my autograph only a couple of times in Rebel Shout but I certainly didn't expect to be signing any in this place.

"Sure, no problem," I jumped down from the stage to join

them. I took the book from Robbie and wrote that I hoped he'd had a great holiday and signed my name below it. As I handed them back to him the lady stepped back from us holding a mobile phone in her hand.

"Is it okay to take a photo?" she asked, smiling.

"Yeah, of course." We turned to face her and I put my arm around Robbie's shoulders as we posed. Just as the photo was taken Robbie turned his head and planted a wet kiss on my cheek making us all laugh.

"Thank you so much, it's way past his bedtime so we're gonna be off now, come on Robbie, thanks again," she ushered him away.

I bid them both farewell and watched for a second as they made their way, hand in hand towards the exit. Robbie turned and gave me a last wave before they made their way out through the door. I waved back, climbed back onto the stage and turned towards the dressing room door. As I looked up, Gina was stood in the doorway. In her long black dress she looked momentarily like a gangster's moll from some film standing in the half light. The smile on her face was warm as I approached.

"Well, looks like someone made a friend."

"Yeah, cute kid, he wanted my autograph would you believe?"

"I saw. It was lovely to watch actually, especially when he gave you that kiss, bless him."

"Well, never turn down a kiss, I say."

"Unless you're in prison."

"Er, I guess so."

Despite my inner turmoil throughout the first set the other

three members seemed content that it had gone well enough.

"Who's up for an opening night celebratory glass of fizz or two later then?" asked Leon.

"Deffo," said Wayne.

Gina looked across at me and we nodded in unison.

When we left the stage after the second set, I felt like a different man, my fears and paranoia had completely melted away. Panic attack over, I felt relaxed as I looked out and across at the audience. As I did, it struck me that around seventy per cent of the people in this room were not actually watching the band at all. This was a stark contrast to when I played live with Rebel Shout, we were the sole focus of the room, everybody watched us, that was kind of the point, wasn't it? Not so much here. Sure, the dance floor was full but we were little more than musical wall flies providing the songs for this purpose. Many did offer generous applause between songs, so we were not entirely unappreciated. For me though, it was a very strange contrast, and one I'd need to get used to.

When the show did come to an end, Gina bid the audience goodnight and we left the stage once more for the dressing room. From there we all agreed to go our separate ways to get changed and reconvene half an hour later in the staff garden area.

As I unlocked the creaky door of my cabin, fumbled for the light switch and walked in, I stood for a moment looking at myself in the tall mirror on the wall by my bed. Dressed in my stage clothes, it still looked like a total stranger staring back at me. This time though I smiled at the absurdity of how I looked with new confidence. I could do this. Fuck it, I was doing this.

I changed into a plain, black, long sleeve t-shirt and cargo shorts, then headed off to meet the others. I arrived to see the three of them sat round a table in the otherwise deserted staff garden. They were already laughing about something together as I approached, their faces lit by a flickering lantern in the table centre.

"Hey, here he is, our new six-string king!" Leon shouted as I pulled up a chair.

"May I pour you a glass of Prosecco, young man?" Wayne offered as he reached down for the bottle.

"You most certainly may, thank you!" I replied taking the glass from him. I smiled at Gina. She had changed into blue denim shorts and a vest top with a cardigan hanging loose over her shoulders. Even this simple outfit seemed to accentuate her figure. She could probably have turned up wearing an old potato sack and still looked good.

"Well on behalf of Wayne and myself we'd like to propose a toast and say well done on your first night with us you two, Gina love, you sang like a diva, and Mac you played like a star, cheers!"

"Cheers, I was a little shaky in the first set, sorry, I pulled it together after, I'm just getting used to all this, you know?"

"Understood Mac, I don't suppose you had quite so many grannies dancing in the audience in your last band," laughed Wayne.

"No, I see now why you have a defibrillator on standby in here."

Pretty soon we were all laughing and getting on like a house on fire. As the drinks flowed, conversational inhibitions were lowered as we sought to dig a little deeper in finding out more about each other. I knew sooner or later, inevitably someone would ask a certain question of me. It turned out to be Leon.

"So, anyway Mac, what's a chart-topping pop star like you doing a gig in a place like this for?"

Back to reality.

"Well firstly I'm not a pop star, if I was I think you'd have heard of me before I showed up here. As for chart topping, we did one single that scraped the charts, that's it, and that was mostly the reason the record company tore up our contract straight after."

"Bloody hell, that sounds a bit harsh, actually we only knew you were in a pop band for a while, that's all Graham told us."

"And I'd never heard of you to be honest," added Gina.

"I expect I could still rustle you up a signed CD if you like?" I smiled sarcastically.

"Nah, you're alright, I'm stuck hearing you every night from now on as it is, don't think I need bonus Mac on CD thanks," she teased.

"So what made you head for the bright lights of Edmouth as your next move, Gina?"

Wayne probed.

"Simple economics, Wayne. I was broke, unemployed and my girlfriend had just kicked me out of her flat so I had to move back in with my mum. This opportunity came up and, well, at least I didn't need to learn a new trade to take it, even though, no offence, it's the polar opposite of what I was doing."

"None taken. Plenty of time to get back to chasing the

dream after this, anyway, right?"

"Well, I think the rock star ship might have sailed for me already, but thanks anyway." The table fell momentarily silent as everyone digested this. I took advantage of the moment to shift the spotlight onto someone else.

"Anyhow, with a voice like hers, if any one of us should be riding high as a pop star it's this girl sat next to me."

Gina shook her head as she picked up her wine glass to take a sip.

"Definitely not. Not interested, never have been."

"How come? Didn't you ever want to be famous?"

"Christ no, fame is the last thing I'd want, I'd hate to have strangers and weirdos coming up to me all the time, a lot of my life's been spent avoiding people, I can't imagine anything worse than fame."

"But you've such a lovely voice, love," said Wayne.

"That's sweet of you to say, thank you, but as soon as I knew I could sing well enough to carry a tune I was thankful enough that I could make a living out of it to be honest and that's enough for me. I've been doing clubs and holiday camps for the last few years, I love the fact that I can go travel wherever in the country I want to and I'm not stuck working in some shithole factory in the same shithole town my whole life. Sorry if that makes me sound stuck up but it's true."

"Hey, you're preaching to the choir here love. Exactly why me and Wayne have been doing the same for years, nothing wrong with that." Wayne took the wine bottle and topped us all up with the last of it.

"One last one for the road, it's late and I can hear bed calling me," said Wayne.

"Suits me," Leon yawned.

"So, how long have you two been together?" asked Gina.

"Ooh, that'll be eleven years in September."

"We first met playing in a wedding band together before we got together as a couple. Then about three years ago we got married on a beach in Lanzarote, oh it was really lovely and dead romantic wasn't it love?"

"Happiest day of my life. Play together, gay together, stay together, that's us," Wayne slurred.

"Right Mister let's get you home. Goodnight you kids, great first show, let's do it all again tomorrow, yeah?"

"Goodnight," we replied in unison. With the happy couple departed this was the first time I found myself alone with Gina. We sat in silence at first, wine glasses in hand, still warm in the summer night heat despite the growing lateness of the hour.

"So what happened with your last girlfriend then?" said Gina finally.

"Alice?"

"Yeah, tell me about Alice."

"Do I have to?" Gina shrugged.

"Might as well."

"Okay, she was pretty, petite, had long black hair and cheated on me like the two timing bitch she was."

"She sounds lovely. Apart from the last bit."

"Yeah a keeper, up to the point where she dumped me and kicked me out of her flat."

"Wait, she dumped you? I thought she was the one doing the two timing?"

"Yes to both, she dumped me and kicked me out to move her new man in, I guess, the one she'd been two timing me with, who just so happened to be the drummer in our band."

"Wow, fuckery on every level."

"Yup."

"And that's why you came here? To get the hell out away from it all?"

"In a nutshell, yes." I sensed the evening was coming to an end but I wanted to get a question or two of my own in before it did. I still knew virtually nothing about her.

"So what brings you to Edmouth, just another job?" Gina nodded.

"Yes, the agency is nationwide so they'll find you work wherever you want. I fancied coming down here to the coast for a summer season. I'm from Surrey way so it's not too far to come."

"I expect your boyfriend misses you." Gina gave a short laugh, most likely at my pathetic attempt at subtlety, or lack of it. She didn't answer though. "No boyfriend then?" I ploughed on in a bid to avoid an awkward silence.

"Nope. Not anymore," she bristled.

"Oh, well sorry to hear that. At least your story can't be as bad as mine." Gina paused to pick up her glass and drank the last of her wine.

"Try worse."

"You're kidding. Wanna tell me about it?"

"Do I have to?"

"Might as well." Gina put her glass back down on the table with a sigh.

"Alright. His name was Richard. We'd been seeing each other for just under two years, living together for the last ten months or so. He was the first boyfriend I thought I could finally call 'serious'. I sang for a living and he was an artist, I really thought we made a perfect match. We seemed... happy. To me anyway. And then, out of the blue, he announced that he'd been seeing someone else and he was leaving me for her." I nodded slowly in sympathy.

"Sad to hear that, awful. I still think finding out Alice was sleeping with our drummer was worse though."

"He left me for my sister. They'd been having an affair for over three months."

"Oh…"

"Yeah, keep it in the family eh? They'd met at the Dragon's sixtieth birthday party, that's my mother by the way, and really hit it off, far better than I knew as it turned out."

I nodded again.

"Okay, you win, that really sucks, sorry."

"I moved out and came here down here as soon as I could. Anyway, on that sour note, I'm off to bed." Abruptly Gina stood up to leave.

"Night Mac."

"Night Gina."

CHAPTER SIX

Although it might have seemed something of an abrupt ending to the night, the somewhat kindred similarities of our circumstances that had brought both Gina and I to Clifton Sands served not only to break the ice but to establish a kind of trust between us. A trust brought about by two people having shared their mutual stories of betrayal and heartbreak. Together we understood each other on a level other's just wouldn't be able to comprehend. Sharing something personal early on somehow lifted a barrier and allowed Gina and I to become friends easily.

Over the course of the next couple of weeks we bonded and spent time in each other's company without any hint of romantic notion. It was nice just to have someone around every day to shoot the shit and get along with, it reminded me just how few friends I really had. Don't get me wrong, Leon and Wayne were great too but Gina and I saw one another every day as well as performing together at night. Not all day, of course, nobody wants to spend that much time together! We fell into a routine of meeting every morning for coffee and breakfast at a local cafe. She was most often the first person I spoke to each day as we met to chat and read the local papers. After that we'd go our separate ways and do our own thing for the rest of the day till we met up again in the evening for showtime.

Things seemed to be settling as just one such morning, around nine thirty as I was shaving, my phone buzzed.

Text from Gina.

'Brew?'

I text back.

'Where are you?'

'Standing outside your door.'

'Stalker. Be out in 5.'

We entered the coffee shop to find it deserted except for a large teenage girl in a sickly green tunic and bulging black leggings seated behind the counter. Her greasy brown hair hung over her eyes which were glued to her phone. She did not look up as we approached the counter opposite her. Her name tag read Jeanette.

"Hi Jeanette!" I beamed.

She looked up slowly and observed us with all the interest of a minimum wage Saturday girl who wished she was anywhere but talking to us.

"Elp ya?"

"Yes, one Americano and one skinny chai latte please," I said smiling pleasantly. I turned to Gina, "Usual table?" Gina nodded an affirmative.

"Name?"

I turned to Jeanette to see her poised with one hand holding a Styrofoam cup and a black marker pen in the other.

"Dalian."

"Eh?"

"Dalian," I repeated, "rhymes with alien."

"Can you spell that?"

"Yes," I replied and paused long enough for her to frown a confused look.

"I meant can you spell it for me?"

"Oh I see yes of course silly me!" I said feigning an embarrassed smile. Gina dug me with her elbow and made her way to the table while trying to hide her own grin. I paid and went over to join her as Jeanette shuffled off to make our drinks.

"That your idea of flirtation?" She smiled as I sat down opposite her.

"Why do you think she fancies me?"

"Not sure you're quite her type."

"Oh... gutted," I replied. I turned and looked out the window next to our table, the sun was beaming. The beach, stony for the best part gave way to soft sand that stretched a long way to the sea now that the tide was out. Light danced and shimmered on the calm ocean, it really wasn't too shabby here, beautiful actually, I liked it.

"What are your plans for the day, G?"

"I'm popping in to see Carlos, then I need to go to Tesco's in town."

"What for?"

"Chocolate and tampons since you ask," she said indignantly.

"No, I meant what do you need to see Carlos for?"

"Oh!" she said blushingly, "He might have some lunch time shifts for me in the bar, you know, extra money and all that."

Carlos was the beefy bar manager in the function room we played in, a large, thirty-something moustachioed guy from Spain. In many ways Carlos was the archetypal Spaniard, with his black hair parted to one side and a little too long to be neat, and of course his loping black moustache hanging down on equal sides of his face. He also had a chunky gold chain round his neck with an actual medallion in the middle.

"He ever strike you as, you know, a bit dodgy?" I asked.

"Carlos? Why do you ask?"

"I dunno, maybe it's the stereotypical Mediterranean cartel style look, let's face it he even looks like Pablo Escobar."

"Pablo Escobar was Colombian."

"Well, of course, yeah I know that," I lied, "but they speak Spanish there don't they, that's what I meant."

"Yeah but… anyway he's not dodgy, he's a good guy, just a bit of a ladies man but I can handle that."

"Right," I answered, wondering what it was exactly she thought she needed to handle. I strolled into town later that morning myself, perusing Edmouth's charity shops as I liked to do, looking for something to read, maybe something by Steven King, there always seemed to be one of his I hadn't read. Then maybe sit on the pier or the beach reading for a couple of hours, even with the summer weather the days could stretch out a little long sometimes when you didn't start you day job till the middle of the evening.

I returned to Clifton in time for lunch, working there entitled me to a twenty five per cent concession on food and drink from the bar menu so to me there was no sense in seeking dining options anywhere else. Lunch trade was lively as I entered, tables filled with trays of fried food to feed the families young and old. Carlos was serving a young couple as I pulled up a wooden stool at the bar and picked up a menu. I don't know why I picked up a menu as the contents hadn't changed since the first day I started.

"May I see the specials board please waiter," I said to Carlos as he turned to me. I sensed Carlos had never particularly liked me, having said that Carlos didn't really seem to particularly like anyone so I didn't take it too personally. That didn't stop me trying to get a rise out of him any time I got the chance though.

"You know we don't have no specials board, Mac."

"The A La Carte menu then?"

"What, you wanna sum ma mamma's a special a paella eh?" He said, humourlessly mocking himself to mock me.

"No thanks, gives me the shits. I'll have a cheese and ham panini please, and a Diet Coke."

"Sure, whatever," he scribbled my order down.

"Elena? Hey Elena where's that milk?

We've got a coffee order waiting here, you go to milk a bloody cow or what?" He barked as he walked away.

"Okay, okay, I'm coming," muttered Elena as she came through carrying a four pint bottle of semi skimmed and emptying it into an urn.

"Oh, hello mister Mac," she said.

I liked Elena, an olive skinned girl with black hair tied back in a tight ponytail, she was a twenty year old Greek exchange student from the island of Kefalonia, working here to earn some money for her studies. She mostly cleaned but helped out wherever there were extra shifts available, doing bar work, table waiting or whatever was on offer, she turned nothing down and I admired her work ethic. Unlike Carlos, who'd clearly lived in England for many years and spoke the adoptive language very well indeed I found Elena's broken English and occasional potty mouthed learnings both funny and endearing.

"Hiya, busy day?" I replied.

"Yeah always," she sighed, "I start at five this morning, finish later in afternoon, I'm like you say, cream crackered?"

"Boss man not working you too hard I hope?" I said nodding towards the back where Carlos had gone.

"Uh huh," she rolled her eyes.

"Do you like Carlos, Elena? I mean... is he friendly to you?"

"Meh, he okay, sometimes," she shrugged. I leaned forwards slightly across the bar towards her.

"Is he ever, you know a bit too friendly?" I said, hoping my meaning wasn't about to get lost in translation. She looked back over her shoulder to make sure she was safe to speak before turning back and leaning in toward me conspiratorially too.

"Well, was one time he get, you know, too close, but I tell him straight out, you touch my butt, I kick your balls!" She whispered.

"Ha ha, good for you girl." I grinned.

Carlos returned to the bar, Elena took a small bottle of spray cleaner and a cloth, then began simultaneously spraying and wiping clean the bar area in round circles.

"You play in your band here tonight mister Mac, or is night off?"

"Yeah we're playing, no rest for the wicked eh?"

"Ah is fun for you, no? All the ladies, they love the guitar man hey?" She teased.

"Ha! He ain't no rock star no more, love! Ha ha ha!" laughed Carlos as he served a pint of lager to a large hairy man in a Union Jack t-shirt with billowing sweat stains under his arms. I decided not to dignify this one with a response, mostly because it was true. Union Jack man turned to me with an alcoholic glaze in his eyes.

He took a slurp of his lager.

"Rock star, eh? Famous are you?" He asked, conversationally, without a trace of sarcasm.

"No."

"Oh…" He nodded. I hoped this might mean the end of this brief conversation, but no.

"My brothers mate once put in a septic tank for David Bowie, you know." I looked back at him.

"Is that a fact? No, I didn't know that. It's a wonderful story though." I said, trying my best to sound sincere.

"Absolute gospel," he nodded before turning away and wondering off to join his family nearby, swaying slightly as he went.

Carlos returned shortly after and banged my lunch plate down on the bar in front of me.

Charming as ever. I picked up the bill on the side of the plate and reached for my wallet to pay.

Inside I took out my bank card but the ID card I needed to produce in order to get my staff discount was gone.

"Er, hey Carlos, look, I think I've lost my ID card."

"Oh no, too bad eh? No card, no discount."

"Well, can't you just put the discount through anyway?"

"Nope. Sorry my friend, I don't make the rules, looks like I have to charge you full price. Better go get yourself a new one."

Arsehole.

With Elena moving away to clear plates and trays from tables, I decided to move away from the bar myself and seek better lunchtime company than Carlos. Looking around I spotted Gina past the hordes of feasting families sitting at a round table by herself. Wearing shorts and a vest top her long bare legs were stretched out in front of her as she basked in the midday sunshine, as I approached I could see she was reading a book through a large pair of brown sunglasses that seemed to cover the whole top half of her face. As I came closer I saw it was a copy of *Men are from Mars, Women are from Venus*.

"Looking for tips?" I said sitting myself down across the table from her.

"Mmm, no not really," she said without looking up, "most of the men I know can be summed up in round about five subjects."

"Oh? And what might they be?"

She sat back, put her book on her lap and paused to consider her answer. "Beer, Sex, Cars, Sports and Curry. In short, men, fundamentally, are easily pleased. Simple creatures with simple, unfussy needs."

"That's an outrageous generalisation Gina, come on."

"No its not, seriously, how many of your mates would define the perfect evening as going out to the pub, drinking with their pals while watching football on Sky Sports and discussing leather seats and alloy wheels, going for a late night curry, then home to give the missus one before passing out?"

"Well okay, I've had worse nights admittedly, but hey, I'm not like that, I hate football, and I play a musical instrument don't forget, that means I'm creative, I have artistic sensitivity."

"No, that comes under sex."

"What? How so?"

"You play the guitar. It is essentially a penis extension. When you're up on stage catching all the eyes of the females in the audience you're basically holding a musical phallus and masturbating."

"Who's masturbating, that sounds interesting?" Leon interrupted as he appeared with Wayne.

"Me apparently, Gina just called me a wanker."

"Only metaphorically, in this instance at least," she smiled as she returned to her book. I finished my lunch and decided I had better go sort a new ID card straight away. As I walked I started thinking about how this job really wasn't as bad as I thought it would be. In fact, apart from Carlos being Carlos just now, I was really quite enjoying my time here but unbeknown to me, dark clouds were gathering on the horizon. Something wicked was coming this way, or to be more precise, someone.

CHAPTER SEVEN

I made my way back across the camp towards reception. It was always nice to see Chloe on the reception desk with that bright and cheerful smile of hers. She and I always had a chat and a laugh whenever our paths crossed, taking the piss out of Graham on the sly mostly. She and her fiancé Simon had even come to see the band a couple of times which was nice. Simon was one of those 'nicest guy you could ever wish to meet', impossible to dislike kind of fellas. Once we got talking it turned out we were into more or less the same type of music. He was absolutely gobsmacked to learn that I had been in Rebel Shout, not only had he bought the single but had actually been to one of our gigs, a fleapit dive in Hackney we'd played one rainy night. Not one that stuck in my memory I have to say, apart from it being a shithole, but Simon said he'd really enjoyed it and genuinely believed we had potential. Most of the time I tried to steer conversation away from my life in London. Still, always nice to meet a fan. Bloody rare too. Chloe on the other hand had never heard of us, by her own admission her taste in music didn't extend much beyond karaoke nights with the girls or whatever cheesy floor filler was playing at Samson's night club in town, as long as she and her friends could dance to it they were happy.

Today must have been Chloe's day off, however, as I pushed through the entrance door to see someone different sat in her chair. As I walked towards the desk a much older woman with tightly permed white hair was typing furiously between squinty looks at a monitor in front of her. Her head appeared to resemble a cauliflower, I smirked a little.

"Hi there," I said.

"Yes? Can I help you?" She looked up irritably. There didn't appear to be anything bright or cheerful about this woman. I clocked her name tag, it read Joyce Garner. I presumed her to be Graham's wife.

"Hi, yes sorry, I play in the house band but unfortunately I'm afraid I seem to have lost my ID card."

"And I suppose you want a new one?" She sighed. No, I just thought I'd swing by and give you the big fucking news, vegetable head.

"Please," I smiled. She let out her breath and rolled her eyes at the same time as if I'd just asked her to type out the entire works of William Shakespeare for me.

"As if I don't have enough to do." She grumbled under her breath. With that Joyce reached under the desk, pulled out a notepad and dropped it down on the surface in front of her. "Last name?"

"McIntyre."

"First name?"

"Dalian."

"Rhymes with alien," came a voice behind me. I turned round expecting to see Gina. It wasn't. It was Alice. "Hello Mac."

"What are you doing here?" I couldn't hide my nervousness.

"I'm here for the weekend, thought I'd get out of London for a bit."

"Really..."

"Yeah, you know, relax, sunbathe, get some sea air. It's good to see you."

"Is it? Funny, you don't seem too surprised to see me Alice, why do I get the feeling this isn't a coincidence?"

"Excuse me! I'm so very sorry to interrupt," drawled Joyce sarcastically, "you can collect your card at two o'clock."

I looked back at Alice.

"Look, is there somewhere we can go to talk?" She said quietly.

Edmouth's vast promenade was awash with holidaymakers, it encompassed a coming together of people of all ages and races, creating a cultural vibrancy and mutual joy seemingly unique to a hot day at the seaside. It was, after all, the place where people came to be happy and enjoy themselves. It was buzzing. All of which I was oblivious to as I walked amongst them with Alice.

For a while neither of us spoke, instead she seemed happy just to take in her new surroundings, the paddle boarders on the sea, the volleyball game on the beach, the multi-coloured row of beach huts along the front, and the small children in sun hats having sun cream rubbed into their tiny lily white limbs. Across the street the hordes of sun worshippers refreshed themselves in the bars, restaurants, cafés and ice cream parlours as the distant screams of teenage thrill seekers, plummeting up and down the giant rollercoaster, echoed from the funfair further down.

My brain was racing as to why Alice had come here. I'd

no doubt it was way too much of a coincidence to be, well, a coincidence. What did she want from me? I had to admit I was intrigued, at least to hear. I certainly couldn't deny how my heart had leapt and skipped a beat upon turning round and seeing her standing there. Dressed in a black Ramones t-shirt, denim cut off shorts and white Converse trainers, she still looked every bit the north London girl I'd met and fallen in love with. As I looked at her she still glowed in an angelic way, I had spent the past couple of weeks trying to push her out of my brain and now I couldn't help but still feel attracted to her. I felt pathetic.

"You must be enjoying yourself here, it's really nice isn't it, very cosmopolitan?" she said at last.

"Not too shabby I suppose," I replied.

Before either of us could say anything else a little boy running across in front of us tripped and sprawled on the ground, his pink ice cream flying out of his hand and splattering on the hot concrete ahead of him. His mother followed up behind him, pushing a further two, smaller children in a pushchair.

"Oh for gawd sake Troy, you know mummy ain't got no more money for annuver one!" She whined, having to raise her voice above the child's anguished sobs. I reached for the change in my jeans pocket and found a two pound coin. I stepped forward and held it out to him.

"Here you go, kiddo. Don't let it spoil your holiday, eh?" I said, nodding to his mum to check this was okay.

"Aw, thanks sweetheart, you're a diamond!"

"That was sweet of you, you always did have a kind heart."

"I'll claim it back on expenses." I deadpanned.

We stopped and leaned on the rail that separated the promenade from the beach and looked out at the sea.

"So come on Alice, you wanted to talk, so tell me, why are you here? And how did you know where to find me?"

"I wanted to see you, and yes I did want to talk…"

"So why not call or text me?"

"I tried, but it seems you've changed your number." I nodded. Oh yeah, I had, I'd forgotten about that. I'd changed it not long before I came here, only a handful of people actually had my new one. I didn't do social media so fair enough maybe I was hard to get hold of.

"I called your parents' house, your Dad answered," she continued. You're lucky it wasn't my mum, I thought. "He was frosty at first of course, and very reluctant to tell me where you were, but I told him I really needed to speak to you. He wouldn't give me your number, but he told me you were doing a summer season playing in a band down here. I thought he was having me on at first…" She trailed off. Her saying it out loud made me squirm with embarrassment.

"It's paid work, okay? That's all." I defended myself.

"Sure, it's okay, I wasn't judging."

A brief lull in conversation followed. I decided to up the ante.

"So where's your boyfriend then? Has he joined you on your merry little trip?"

"I don't have a boyfriend. Lance and I are no longer together," she stared at the floor.

"Oh dear, that's a shame. Fatal accident was it?"

"That's not very nice, Mac."

"Nor is sleeping with your boyfriend's mate behind his back." Straight for the jugular.

"Look, I… I made a mistake…"

"A mistake? Oh no… no Alice," my temper began to rise along with my voice. "A mistake is when you get a loaf of brown bread from the shop when you meant to get white. There was no mistaking what you were doing all that time behind my back was there Alice?"

"Mac, wait, please…" I was on a roll now. I turned to face her full on.

"You come waltzing down here like butter wouldn't melt in your mouth, expecting it all to be fine and dandy between us, and for what Alice, eh? You were going to let me walk out of that flat thinking it was just me that was making you unhappy. You weren't going to tell me it was Lance, were you? Tell me the truth, you weren't were you?"

"Mac…"

I still wasn't done. All the pain, hurt and upset from her betrayal all came flooding back at once to engulf me in a vitriolic tsunami of anger. I raged on.

"Because I'd say you didn't just burn your bridges, you practically blew them up with bloody dynamite. All that time you were carrying on behind my back I never suspected anything because I trusted you Alice, because I loved you, and stupidly I thought you loved me, and all the time you were with him. Getting, getting, bloody lanced, by Lance!" I practically shouted the last bit. People around us looked up. I didn't care. Alice burst into tears, turned and ran back in the direction of the camp. My anger deflated like a balloon. Well, come on, she deserved to hear that. Somehow, I still felt guilty, she still had that hold on me.

Two little boys eating candy floss in dirty t-shirts stood staring at me from the space behind where Alice had just vacated.

"Hey, she had that coming didn't she?" I asked.

Both of them stared vacantly at me. Their mum and dad quickly came over to usher them away. I sighed deeply and slowly turned to follow Alice back in the direction of the camp.

When I finally reached the entrance it occurred to me that I still did not know the reason why Alice had come here. Not that I'd actually given her much of a chance to explain herself, or even get a word in edge ways amid my ranting. With my anger now subsided, perhaps it was time to exercise a little diplomacy.

As I wandered through camp, there were people coming and going everywhere, I was beginning to think this was hopeless, she could be anywhere in this place. A glance to my left however and I spotted her. She was sat alone on a wooden bench beneath the shade of a cluster of scrawny looking trees. I didn't know if she had deliberately made herself quite so easy to find or not, perhaps in the hope I would come after her.

I left the crowded concrete pathway and stepped onto the lawn area to make my way over to her. I could see Alice had stopped crying but her eyes would not meet mine as I approached the bench. For a brief second I stood, not quite sure of myself, before turning round and taking the seat next to her. Unsure again of quite how to proceed from here I didn't say anything for a while, the silence between us only broken by Alice's occasional post tearful sniffing.

My eyes fell on some seemingly recent graffiti crudely scrawled into the woodwork on the seat space between us. It read:

Be here Wednesdays at 10pm and I'll suck it.

I couldn't help wondering if this message had been left for someone specific or freely offered to whoever in general. Either way I worked Wednesday nights. I swiftly rejected the idea of asking Alice if she'd written it, by way of a humorous ice breaker. Alice sniffed an extra loud sniff and I took my cue.

"So what did happen between you and Lance?" I asked in a softer voice.

"What do you care?"

"Just asking."

"Why, so you can humiliate me some more?" I stayed quiet this time. Alice was not going to get any sort of apology from me. We were a long, long way from being over what had gone before, or at least I was. Possibly we never would be.

"He was screwing some tart if you must know. I dumped him the moment I found out. I'm sure you won't be sorry to hear it."

That was true. I can't say I was surprised either. Lance had always been loose with his morals and able to find a warm bed wherever he wanted. I think that was part of the reason he wanted to be in a band, for the attention. Girls. Groupies, or anything with a pulse, that was his motto. He was just one of those sort of blokes, fidelity just didn't seem to suit him.

"I see," I said, still unable and unwilling to offer her a single word of solace. How could I? It was all much too close to home. "I hear he joined a new band?" Alice nodded, looking up at me for the first time.

"Yeah, pretty much straight after you guys got dropped he heard that Rat Salad were looking for a new drummer and he auditioned."

Well... well... well... so he'd started feathering himself a new nest before Rebel Shout had even broken up then. I guess it wasn't just my girlfriend he was shafting behind my back, it was me too, not to mention Jase. You think you know someone, the backstabbing bastard. Rat Salad, I had to admit were a decent band, we knew these boys, they were a four piece, a little more of a rock act than us, with two female backing singers. They were on more or less the same circuit as us and had a really big following.

"Rat Salad, eh? Lucky boy Lance. They're not signed though are they?"

"Not yet but it's only a matter of time, they've been picked up by some American management, they've got a West Coast tour booked as support act starting in LA next month."

"Wow..." I said in spite of myself. It was impossible not to feel a certain amount of jealousy, as well as the sinking feeling that we'd had our chance and that our ship had sailed.

"Yeah, all very exciting, till I found out he was sticking it to Tilly, that bony little bitch of a backing singer," spat Alice bitterly. So there it was. This conversation was certainly proving to be an enlightening one.

"Yeah well, all men are bastards aren't they?" I looked across the camp and let that one linger in the air. I sensed the words were not lost on Alice as she gathered herself.

"Mac, please don't start shouting at me again when I say this but when I said I'd made a mistake I didn't mean sleeping with Lance behind your back. Yes I know what I did was appalling and despicable, and I know that I hurt you in a way that means you'll probably never be able to forgive me." I turned to look at her, she had closed the gap between us and was staring intensely at me. All trace of her earlier tears were gone from her dark brown eyes now, the seductive allure I'd known before however, had not. "The mistake I made was being so stupidly blinded enough as to choose the wrong man over the wonderful, kind one I already had."

Bullshit.

"Ha, yeah right, and you wouldn't be saying this because you've just found out he's an arsehole and dumped him?"

"I don't expect you to forgive me Mac, like I said. I know you'd never take me back anyway after I was such a bitch to you." I stared back into those hypnotic eyes and wished to god I could believe her. I chose to look away again in order to break the spell but I couldn't help now finding myself feeling a conflicted. I should be elated at her declaration that there was a chance we would be getting back together yet I felt despondent to hear her say it instead. I felt disgusted by the recent memory of her cheating on me. Yet, my heart leapt at the notion of a potential reconciliation. It's a fine line between love and hate alright.

"I screwed up Mac, I know. I can't take back what I did, but I may be able make amends in one small way. That's the reason I came here." So, here we were, finally down to the nitty gritty.

"Go on," I was genuinely intrigued. She took a deep breath.

"I was walking through Camden Market a couple of weeks ago when I bumped into Maddy, it was a bit awkward between us at first, to be honest I don't think she would have even acknowledged me but for the fact she was very keen to ask me about you. She wanted to know if I'd been in contact or seen you, cos Jase was wanting to get hold of you. I told her I hadn't."

"Hang on. Why didn't Jase just text or call me himself?"

"Oh Mac, keep up! You changed your number, remember?" She rolled her eyes. Her old self seemed to be returning.

"Oh right... So what did Jase want?"

"According to Maddy he's been writing and demoing some new songs, she says they're the best stuff he's ever done. He's sent them out to different record companies and he's got serious interest already." I was impressed and happy for Jase. I secretly knew he would never be able to settle down and work for his old man. "They want him to get some musicians together so he can showcase his new material and ultimately be the new band. I guess you can join the dots from here, he needs a guitarist and you're his first choice Mac."

"Oh shit…" I puffed out my cheeks. I didn't see this one coming. Just as I'd settled into a total change of lifestyle.

"You've still got Jase's number I take it?" I nodded. "Call him. It could really be another chance for you, Mac, a second chance." I didn't know what to say, it was a lot to process at once. Alice stood up. "Well, I said I wanted to make some sort of amends, I hope I have, I owed you. Looks like my work here is done, I guess."

All of a sudden she looked vulnerable. I stood up next to her and met her gaze. Quickly she leaned in and kissed me lightly on the cheek.

"Goodbye, Mac. Good luck," she whispered. Her eyes began to well up again as she walked away.

"Alice! Alice, wait!" I called after her. She stopped and looked back at me. "Thank you."

She smiled and went to turn away again. "At least stay tonight, you could watch the band, we could have a drink together after if you'd like?"

A pause.

"You'd really like to have a drink with me? Thought you'd want me gone again as quickly as possible."

"Well, just to say thanks. You're here now…"

"Okay, I suppose I do have accommodation booked here till tomorrow anyway. Are you sure Mac? Really?"

"Sure. Might even stretch to a packet of pork scratchings too if you're lucky."

"You know how to treat a girl," she laughed. "I'll go freshen up and see you later, yeah?"

She headed off in the direction of the chalets, almost skipping.

CHAPTER EIGHT

For the rest of the day all I could think about was Alice. As we were getting ready for the show, every corner of the dressing room somehow reminded me of her. As dressing rooms go it was pretty drab and not especially large. Painted in a dreary, nondescript matt grey with a single double window closed off by a pair of heavily lined, mildew smelling curtains. It had an air of claustrophobia about it that always had us keen to get the hell out and onto the stage. The only furniture was an old brown leather Chesterfield sofa, on which sat Leon and Wayne as they argued over the choice of colour scheme with which to paint the kitchenette of their flat. Opposite them were two faded cream armchairs, both unoccupied, while in the middle sat a cheap black ash coffee table with multiple round coffee mug rings, a handful of magazines and newspapers that nobody ever read. Across the other side of the room against the far wall, in front of a large dressing table mirror surrounded by light bulbs sat Gina, applying her eye makeup and occasionally spraying product on her hair. Various different sized bottles, sprays, tubes and make-up tubs crowded the desk in front of her. Yet, all I could think about was her.

"Penny for your thoughts, McIntyre," Gina startled me.

"What? Oh, no, save your money, nothing going on here, I was just, you know, getting ready, getting into the zone."

I hadn't mentioned Alice of course. The situation seemed way too complicated to open up for public discussion.

"You seem a little preoccupied," she probed. How is it females always seem to have some kind of intuitive nose for sensing when something has happened?

"Nope, just getting ready to rock 'n roll, baby."

The buzzer alerted us on stage. Saved by the bell. It had certainly been the most unexpected of unexpected days. At the start of it, Alice had been the girl who'd not only stolen my heart but had laughingly plunged a dagger of betrayal into it. The last person I ever wanted to have clapped eyes on again. The Whore of Babylon. Now she was joining me for a drink tonight, at my invitation. Fucked up or what? I promised myself two drinks with Alice and then she was gone. Just to say thank you. She had, after all come all this way down here from London to give me information that might just change my life.

As the lights went down moments later, we took to the stage as Gina stepped into the spotlight. As she began her nightly routine, I tried desperately not instantly scan the room to seek out you know who. Instead, I restricted myself to nonchalantly glancing around. Alice wouldn't be seen dead on this dance floor, I knew that for a fact. I lasted till about the third song in before I had a ludicrously panicking thought that perhaps she might have changed her mind, having thought better of it, and gone home on the train after all. I looked up. The place was heaving, with every table in the room occupied behind the now full dance floor and a packed bar area. It was at the far end of the bar that I finally spotted her. Alice stepped out from the shadow and leaned into the bright lights of the bar as my eyes looked in that direction. She smiled, knowing I'd now seen her.

Oh, that smile.

I was instantly transported back to that hot, sweaty night in Camden. She'd smiled that same smile that hooked me then, and god help me she was doing it again now. Remembering that night, I missed everything about being in a band, a real band that is, not this cabaret stuff. I missed creating and performing new music, looking out from a stage and seeing a sea of front row faces, all sweating and jumping around. I missed being at the heart of the music scene, being relevant. Being who I really was.

"Can I get you a drink, handsome?" I fought through the crowds at the bar to reach her during the interval. She was sat, one leg crossed over the other, on a bar stool, wearing a short yellow cotton sundress with sunflowers on it, that complimented her long black hair perfectly. She looked beautiful.

"Allow me, please my lady," I replied with mock gallantry.

"Go on then, vodka and lime thanks," she smiled.

"Mac, grab me a bottle of sparkling water while you're ordering will you?" shouted Gina as she approached us. "Oh, sorry, I didn't mean to interrupt."

"No, no it's fine, er… Gina, meet, er… this is Alice."

Gina's eyes widened, she smiled at Alice then back at me. "Oh, hi!"

"Hi," Alice replied with a cold smile.

"I've heard all about you," returned Gina breezily. I wanted to stamp on her foot. Alice's smile faded.

"Right, well I'll see you back onstage in a bit then, eh?" I quickly ushered her away.

"Nice to meet you!" called Gina, disappearing back into the crowd.

Alice rolled her eyes.

"Well, cheers!" I said, handing Alice her drink.

"I see my reputation has preceded me."

"Well, I had mentioned the breakup in conversation naturally…"

"It's alright, I'm sure whatever you told them it was deserved," she sighed, staring down at her glass with resignation.

Infuriatingly, one of the male punters at the bar suddenly decided to engage me by asking me all sorts of tedious questions about my guitar. I tried to keep my answers as short and blunt as possible in the hope he'd get the hint but I couldn't get away from him, the relentless 'techie' questions just kept coming. I wanted to break a bottle over his head to shut him up. I was acutely aware of Alice sitting at the other side of me, silently being ignored. When I finally turned away from him interval time was up.

"Alice, do you fancy a bite to eat later?

There's a nice Italian place down the road its open late, I've not been but it's meant to be nice, what do you say?"

Italian had always been her favourite food. She looked up and smiled warmly.

"That would be lovely, Mac."

As the band reconvened back in the odorous backstage room Gina sidled over to me.

"Oh my god, that was her wasn't it? What on earth is she doing here? Don't tell me you and Cruella Deville are getting back together?"

"Back off Gina," I snapped. "I don't appreciate your little comments either. You don't even know her."

"Oh I am sorry," she said sarcastically, but slightly wounded. "I was kind of under the impression you hated her guts, I was a bit surprised to see you suddenly cosying up to each other at the bar, that's all?"

"We weren't and it's… it's complicated okay? I don't owe you or anyone else an explanation, so leave it alone Gina, alright?"

"Whoa, easy up Romeo, I wasn't asking for one, I don't care what you do, just don't come crying when it's your butt that gets bitten once again."

Gina and I made no eye contact for the remainder of the show, happy to ignore each other throughout. I've never been so glad to see the end of a gig, my guitar was back on its stand and I was leaving the stage at the end of the last song before Gina had even said goodnight to the audience, something that clearly didn't go unnoticed by Leon and Wayne as I felt their eyes on me. Tonight I didn't care.

I met with Alice and suggested we head off to the restaurant right away, I suddenly felt the need to be away from Clifton Sands, somewhere neutral, anywhere else but this place. After a short walk we quickly found the Italian restaurant, Milano's.

The place was busy and clearly popular but we were seated immediately. I ordered a bottle of Chianti from the wine list. The rear of the room was dimly lit creating a romantic intimacy. Alice's beauty grew under the candlelight. We ordered, chatted about our respective lives following on from when we last saw each other. We were both careful not to bring anything up that would ruin the dinner. We were already on the second bottle of red wine, the earlier evening stresses and strains having all but melted away to leave me feeling relaxed.

Later, with both of us far too full to even contemplate dessert, I paid the bill and we left.

Outside, the summer night air was hot with the white full moon shimmering on the sea waves as we strolled along the promenade back towards the camp. Alice linked her arm in mine and placed her head on my shoulder.

"Thank you Mac, thank you for a lovely meal, I've really enjoyed seeing you again."

"It's been nice to see you too, Alice," I breathed. Now, for the first time in the evening my mind turned to how this evening could end. My thoughts now wavered between the two obvious options. We walked the remainder of the distance mostly in silence until we were stood outside Alice's chalet.

"This must be your penthouse then."

"Yup, this is me," she nodded. "You know, it was actually good to see you up onstage again Mac, music aside obviously, it brought back memories seeing you up there."

"Likewise seeing you in the audience," I smiled. She smiled back and leaned in closer to me. She gently took my head in her hands and kissed me with a passionate intensity that set every fibre in my body tingling with excitement. I did my best to return the favour as I slid my hands around her slender waist and felt the heat of her skin beneath the thin cotton material of her dress. I pulled her closer. Abruptly she pulled back, breaking the embrace. She took a half step backwards.

"Come back with me, Mac."

"What?"

"Come back to London with me, on the train tomorrow morning."

"Back to London?"

"Back to my flat, you can move back in with me, we can make a fresh start, you and me, you can join up with Jase's new band and really get your life back together, you can leave all this behind, everything will be just like it was before, only better this time."

"Wait, Alice, hold on, I've got a job here, commitments. I can't just up and walk out."

"'Yes you can. What are they gonna do, sue you? Sure, they'll be pissed, you'll probably have one or two shitty messages on your voicemail but they're agency run, right? They'll just call them up and you'll be replaced in a matter of days. Cabaret muso's are two a penny Mac, in a week or two you'll be all gotten over and forgotten."

Alice had clearly thought this through. The sharp focused clarity now in her eyes contrasted directly with the alcoholic bleariness in mine.

"Alice, I can't just let people down like that. I like those people, they've been good to me."

"They'll get over it. They don't matter Mac, can't you see what you need?" She took my hand. "We have a chance here to put the past behind us and start a whole new beginning together Mac, right here, right now. A fresh start, a new band and I promise I will never hurt you again." She touched my face and kissed me again, this time she was gentle. Then she turned and unlocked her chalet door before looking back at me.

"If you don't want to be with me Mac, then I'll understand, but my train goes at nine in the morning and I want more than anything for you to be on it with me when it leaves. It's up to you, Mac. See you at the station. I hope."

With that she slowly blew me a kiss, stepped inside the now opened door. As I made my way back across camp, the alcohol had begun to wear off but I was still somewhat in a daze. What was crystal clear however, was Alice's seemingly now or never, one time proposition. Her offer was simple. Cut all my ties here tonight and leave in the morning train to live happily ever after. Except, of course, it wasn't that simple. Clifton Sands had been there to offer me salvation when I was at my lowest. I'd come here fresh faced, willing and without any expectations but I'd found friendships here. They certainly did not deserve to have me walk out on them in this way and be treated like this. Now there was Alice. At the end of the day what was done was done, nothing could change that, and it very much was the end of the day. All that was left now was forgiveness. Or not. Forgive and forget, there's a phrase for you.

Could I forgive Alice? My immediate future depended entirely on it. I had to weigh up what I had to lose by leaving here with what I had to lose by staying.

There had to be only one answer, and I'd already made up my mind.

CHAPTER NINE

As I strolled out of the gates of Clifton Sands Holiday Camp the following morning, the birds harmonised with the glowing sun. I made my way towards the train station to meet Alice in complete serenity. I felt calm now. Calm and confident that I was very much making the right decision. The right choice for me. I crossed over the street and stood at the station entrance. I paused and looked back over my shoulder towards Edmouth seafront. I looked up at the timetable screen. The train to London was on time. No delays. I made my way to the platform. I heard Alice shout my name as she came over towards me, she was dressed in black jeans, black vest top and blue denim jacket. She was carrying a brown leather Gucci travel bag. She looked great, as always. Her smile was literally from ear to ear.

"Mac! Mac! Over here! Oh my god, for a while I thought you weren't gonna come, but thank god…Where's your case?"

Her smile faltered.

"I'm not coming with you, Alice."

"What?"

"I'm not coming back to London with you."

"Why? Look, we can always get a later train if it's a problem…"

"I'm staying here." A look of anger flashed across her creased brow, then she caught herself to gain composure.

"Hey Mac, come on baby, I know it's a big step but don't go getting cold feet on me, this is our future, this is you and me…"

"But it's not about you and me is it Alice?" I looked directly into her eyes. "It's about you. It's always been about you, hasn't it. You planned all this didn't you? All of it, coming down here with the big show of remorse, the crocodile tears, the big favour to patch things up, and finally the big seduction to seal the deal."

"I don't know what you're talking about. You're being ridiculous Mac, why would I do that?"

"Because when we first got together you got your first taste of what being with me could do for you. I can't blame you for that really, what girl wouldn't want a rock star boyfriend, eh? If I got rich and famous what would that mean to you? All that money, the lifestyle, shopping sprees, travelling round the world, top hotels, big houses, flash sports cars… Sounds amazing doesn't it. You'd never have to work again that's for sure."

"Yeah and so what? What's wrong with that? You think I want to work in a fucking bank my whole life?" She hissed.

"There's nothing wrong with that. Nothing at all. Nothing except you don't care who you have to screw to get there. Alice, you ditched me the moment I became redundant and worthless to you. You didn't waste any time jumping into bed with Lance when you found out he could whisk you away to LA. Only it didn't work out did it? You didn't dump Lance did you Alice? He dumped you didn't he?"

Alice glared at me in silence.

"Bet you forgot, I know Lance. I know exactly what he's like, so you were back to square one then weren't you, right up until you bumped into Maddy and found out all about Jase and his new prospects. Then, light bulb moment, you knew what to do. Give old Mac a call. Come act like the hero. Come save me from the seaside suicide. Only Alice, I know you too. I know exactly what you're like." She shook her head. "It nearly worked Alice, you almost had me, hook, line and sinker. Almost. Then I woke up this morning and it was like all the fog had cleared from my mind and I could see you for what you are as clear as day." I laughed. "You're nothing but a player, Alice. Only this time, you lose."

Her eyes looked as though they'd turned black as she exploded into a rage.

"And I'll tell you what you are Mac, shall I? You're a worthless fucking loser! Only a complete moron would turn down what you've been offered, and for what? To stay in some sad, little holiday camp band instead! What a joke you are! It just goes to show, all you'll ever be is a failure!"

An elderly homeless man with long white hair and an even longer, dirty white beard sat up from a station bench where he'd been sleeping, evidently woken by Alice's shouting. Oblivious to the raging storm he shuffled over to her and held an old plastic tub towards her.

"Change?"

"Fuck off out of it, you filthy old skank!"

The man was unphased by her abuse and turned towards me with the cup. I gave him what I had in my pocket. He nodded in thanks.

The trained rolled in. "You know what? I'm just gonna leave you and fucking crystal meth Santa Claus here to get acquainted. Two deadbeat losers together eh?" She sneered.

"Goodbye Alice. Look after yourself won't you? It's what you're best at after all."

Alice flipped me the middle finger, swung her bag over her shoulder and boarded the train without a backwards glance. I watched it disappear into the distance.

The homeless man reappeared and wandered over to the spot where Alice had entered the train. He reached down and picked something up from the platform floor. I recognised it as Alice's purse. She must have dropped it. Clearly only interested in the money, the old man tipped it up and shook out a couple of ten pound notes and a decent handful of change.

"Finders keepers I'd say," I laughed. He gave me a hearty toothless grin and stuffed the money into a dirty coat pocket. As he turned towards the exit he tossed the purse over his shoulder. It flew across the platform and landed on the track. The old man shuffled away towards the exit, the sole of his ancient brown boots had almost completely come away and flapped like a flip flop on the ground as he walked. He paused to look back at me. He grinned with what teeth he had left and saluted towards me. I found myself alone on the deserted platform.

I remained for some time in silence. The calm after the storm. I did feel calm, like a new man in fact. I felt as if somehow, somewhere in the cosmos of my head, the planets had shifted and realigned. A wrong had been righted and now the wicked witch was dead, to me anyway. Closure, finally. I took a deep breath before finally turning and making my way out of the station exit.

I peered through the canteen windows as I made my way

back through the camp, it was by now mid-morning and the breakfast shift was all but done. Only a couple of tables remained occupied, one by a family of five, the only one of which was still eating was a baby boy in a highchair being spoon fed. Sat alone at the other end of the room was a man with his head in his hands. He took a shaky sip of his juice, he was definitely nursing a hangover. The only other person in the room was Elena who was busy cleaning the tables ready for the lunchtime session. Although some might say menial, it was fascinating to watch her at work like this, applying such quick and clinical efficiency to her task. Such was her speed on the job that most of the tables were already finished. As if sensing being watched, she looked up and spotted me through the window.

Immediately, she broke into a wide smile, her brilliant white teeth in perfect contrast to the dark, olive skin. I grinned and waved at her as I started walking away.

I had nearly passed the end of the building when I happened to glance through the very last window. What I saw made me stop and look once again. At the very end of the canteen, stood Gina and Carlos. Their muted gestures looked to be heated. Carlos made an exaggerated shrugging gesture as Gina leaned in towards him, jabbing a finger at his face as she spoke. With that she turned and stormed away towards the canteen exit. Carlos appeared to shout something after her but she ignored him, slamming the door as she left. I stood for a moment in bemusement, staring through into the now empty room and wondering what on earth could have caused such a fiery encounter. Both of them were always ready for a fight, so who knows. I needed to have a word with her myself after last night. A job for another day, I decided. I walked into the gardens.

"Geezar!" I turned around to see a young man with shoulder length dreadlocks in dirty shorts and a vest top sat on the wooden bench opposite me. I realised it was Matthew, the gardener.

"Oh, hi."

"How's it going bud? Take the weight off," he said as he moved his dusty backpack from the seat next to him and gestured for me to sit.

"Don't mind if I do. It's Matthew isn't it? My name's Mac."

Matthew placed the rolled up cigarette he was smoking between his lips and offered his hand out to me.

"Yeah but not even my parents call me that, it's Matt. Only one that calls me Matthew is you know who."

"Ah yes, good old Graham. Everyone's favourite boss. So, you been working here long, Matt?"

"Only since the Spring, started in April. My uncle used to do the job here before me for years, but he hurt his back at the start of the year so he decided to jack it in and take early retirement. I was out of work at the time so he asked me if I wanted to take over, I was desperate for a job so I nearly bit his hand off. Old Graham wasn't too sure, especially when he first clapped eyes on me, but my uncle vouched for me, promised him I wouldn't let anyone down and, well I guess I haven't yet. I'm still here anyways!"

"Doing a good job from what I can see."

"I just keep my head down and get on with it, you know. Works for me."

Looking at Matt now I couldn't help myself but think he looked just like one of those protesters you see on the news, being dragged away by the police having just been forcefully freed with bolt cutters from a tree they'd recently chained themselves to. I was suddenly aware that Matt was giving me a squinty, slightly quizzical look, as if reading my ever so slightly judgemental thoughts. I gave a small cough and smiled blandly back at him in response.

"So anyway, I've heard all about you bud, I was talking to Elena the other day in the canteen, she told me all about this rock star guitar slinging dude we had playing in the house band, that's true right?"

"Well, the part about me being in the house band is."

"Ah now come on, don't be coy," he grinned, "I googled your band, there's not much but it does say you had a song in the charts, She's got it!"

"She's on it!"

"Right. So go on then, what was life in the fast lane like?"

"Brief."

"I bet you've got some stories to tell though, wild parties and that, eh?"

"Well, sometimes we'd all have a second cup of cocoa before bed, it's true."

"Bloody cocoa indeed…" Abruptly he sat forward, reached down to his right and picked up his backpack. He dropped it on his lap, looked to see if the coast was clear and began to unzip it.

"I tell you what bud, I've got some coke in here if you're interested?" He winked.

"No, no way. You've got me all wrong, sorry mate. Time I was going."

"Whoa what's the hurry, it's a hot day, aren't you thirsty?" He pulled out a six pack of Coca Cola cans. I sat back down again, hoping I didn't look quite as stupid as I felt.

"Oh I get it, just cos of how I look I must be a drug dealer right?" I looked him in the eye for a second before I started to realise what was going on.

"You're winding me up aren't you?" Matt laughed.

"Yeah I was just fucking with you, sorry. It's just my way of sizing people up, don't worry!"

"Glad I passed that test with flying colours then."

"Nah you're alright by me any day mate."

"Lucky me."

"Right I'd better get back to the grind," he said standing up and stubbing his roll up out on the path. "Hey, I'm meeting my girlfriend Tam tomorrow at the Dog and Duck at one, why don't you tag along? Tam used to be in a band, she'd love to meet you, whaddaya say?"

"Sure, why not. Tell her she'll only be meeting the guitarist in a holiday camp band though, okay?"

"Don't worry I'll tell her not to ask for your autograph in public!" I instantly liked him, he seemed genuine. I needed to meet a good person after today. "One o'clock, Dog and Duck, be there!"

"First pint is on me!" I replied.

"Adios Amigo."

CHAPTER TEN

I watched until Matt disappeared. I found myself looking forward to tomorrow. As I walked back to my room I spotted Gina coming out of the laundrette. Instead of going over to patch things up I took cover behind a family. She didn't seem to notice me. As I watched her disappear out of sight, I looked over to the coffee shop. I couldn't avoid her. She was my friend, we had spent so many mornings together over a cup of coffee. Why would I waste what we had built together? Especially over someone like Alice.

Twenty minutes later I was following Gina's footsteps towards her chalet, armoured with a peace offering in the name of a skinny chai latte. I was confident we could work it out in no time. As her place came into view, I could see the front door had been propped fully opened.

The late morning sunshine streamed through into the living space. I could see Gina inside and I could hear her radio playing Amy Winehouse as I approached. With her back to me she hummed along as she took items of clothing out of her linen basket and folded them. I tapped the base of the door with my foot.

"Hi."

She was unphased at my arrival.

"Oh, hi." She didn't even bother to look up at me.

"So I was wondering if you had a minute?"

"Not really, no. Bit busy right now."

"Oh, right, I see…" Time to play the peace card. "Hey, I got you a latte if you want it?"

"No thanks."

Shit.

"Look G, I'm sorry about last night okay?"

She turned and offered me the briefest of eye contact before moving over and placing the last items of clothing into a drawer.

"Okay."

"So are you going to bloody ask me in now or what?" Finally, she stopped what she was doing and turned to face me, her hands on her hips.

"Five minutes."

Fine, that'll do it, I thought. Without another word I walked over, sat myself down and placed her drink down on a coaster atop her glass coffee table. I took a long, grateful sip of mine. It tasted good. I relaxed a little, happy just to have made it over the threshold. Gina picked up a tea towel and turned her attention to drying and putting away her pots.

"So, have you come to invite me to the wedding then? I'll wear a hat but I'm not buying you a present."

"No. No wedding, no nothing. We're not getting back together. She's gone and she won't be back, I sent her packing."

"Oh dear, that's a shame."

"No it isn't." That made her smile.

"So why was she here in the first place then? You owe her money or something?"

"She came down to ask me if I'd go back to London with her. Move back in to her flat, like nothing ever happened."

Her frown reappeared. "Oh. Well maybe you should have."

"What's that supposed to mean?" Gina put her tea towel down and turned to face me again.

"Oh come on Mac, I saw the way you two were at the bar last night, gazing at each other like perfect star crossed lovers!"

I looked downwards at my feet, unable to meet her eyes, knowing she was right, that must have been exactly what we looked like. She came over and sat down on the chair next to me.

"So come on then lover boy, what happened? Did you find out she used to be a man or did you spot the 666 on the back of her head?" I looked back up, Gina smiled back.

"Yes, well she might be the daughter of Satan that's true but let's just say she had an ulterior motive for wanting us to get back together. Fortunately, I saw through it all and ended it, once and for all."

I hoped this would be enough to satisfy Gina, I certainly wasn't going to mention the proposed offer of joining Jase's new band. There was no need to open that particular can of worms and besides, I'd faced enough questions on my personal life for one morning.

"Well, for what it's worth I think you made the right choice." She nodded. "So the Alice ship has set sail for evermore then?"

"Yes, and hopefully she'll strike an iceberg and sink too."

"Not that your bitter eh?"

"Actually no, I'm not bitter Gina. I'm just glad my head ruled my heart this time and it's all over." Gina nodded again and stood up.

"Good, well time's up, go on, bugger off now, I need to get

on with stuff." I picked up my cup and made my way to the door.

"Fine. I'm actually pretty busy myself, my sock drawer hasn't been rearranged in days, you should see the state of it."

"One can only imagine. See you tonight."

"Sure will." I stepped out into the bright sunshine.

"Oh and Mac?" I turned round as Gina picked up her drink.

"Thanks for the coffee," she said with a smile and a wink.

After all the ups and downs of the previous evening I wanted for nothing more than a quiet and uneventful night tonight. As far as tonight's musical performance went, the blander and more forgettable the better. I spent the afternoon on my own on the beach, eating ice cream and playing on the two pence machines. I managed to win quite the haul in the sweaty amusements. A red rubber octopus, a small pack of cheap sweets and a garish gold coloured key ring with 'Yo Dawgs' printed on it. While I was proud of my afternoon's work, I decided to give them to a couple of little boys who had been in there all day too.

I was in a cheery mood as I entered the backstage room, freshly showered and changed, in preparation for the show.

"S'up bitches!" I placed my guitar case down on the floor as I entered. I could tell something wasn't right. Wayne was seated in an armchair and I could see he did not look at all well. His eyes were closed, his face sweaty and his skin looked white. Leon and Gina stood either side of him looking worried.

"Uh oh, you okay Wayne? You're looking a bit green around the gills there mate."

"He's been throwing up," Leon answered for him. "Think he might have a touch of food poisoning."

"Oh no, well you can't go on in that state, one of us will have to go get hold of Graham, let him know…"

"No. It'll be fine, I'll get through it."

"Me and Wayne, we don't do cancelling."

No wonder Graham held the pair of them in such high regard, their 'show must go on', 'never say die' attitude towards their profession was both remarkable and admirable.

Nonetheless, going ahead with the performance still didn't seem like a good idea, no one wanted to see the poor old bugger keel over into a puddle of his own sick. Gina and I exchanged worried glances as I walked over towards them. Gina squatted down and placed her hand affectionately on top of Wayne's as she spoke softly to him.

"Listen Wayne darling, we totally get that you're way too proud to consider cancelling and maximum respect to you for that, but the bottom line is you really don't have to do this if you're not up to it, none of us will think any less of you I swear. Besides, Mac and I could probably fill in by doing some of the set as a duo."

I nodded in agreement. Wayne half hiccupped, half coughed suddenly and we all, even Leon, took a half step backwards. Placing his hand on his chest he took a deep breath and opened his eyes.

"No, I'll be okay but I will need a bucket."

Gina stood up and looked at Leon. He nodded and went off to search the cleaning cupboard.

He emerged a short time later with a large stainless steel

bucket, placed it, at Wayne's request, at the back of the stage behind his drum kit. When the time came to go on, Wayne took one last visit to the bathroom.

"Last chance, are you absolutely sure he's gonna be okay up there?"

"I know Wayne, if he says he is, he is."

With the final decision made, we took to the stage and began.

You had to hand it to Wayne, though the style of music we played never required him to perform any kind of Keith Moon style histrionics, it was still impressive. Between each song he had his head in the bucket, but the audience didn't seem to notice. The end of the first set came as a relief to us as much as to him.

"Wow, well done. You legend. That was one shift of a first half." I congratulated him. He fumbled to the dressing room chair looking exhausted, covered in sweat.

"Yes, that was a trooper's performance, bless you, how are you feeling now?" asked Gina. Wayne lifted his hand up and made a side to side waggling motion.

"So, so." At that moment, in what I can only describe as an act of true love, Leon came through the stage door carefully carrying Wayne's almost full to the brim sick bucket.

Gina and I instinctively backed up against the wall as he skipped past us.

"I think it must have been something I ate."

"Babe, it looks like everything you ate," Leon shouted. He re-emerged through the bathroom door with the newly emptied bucket when Wayne groaned loudly, lurched out of his chair and pushed past him.

"Oh dear, are you going to be sick again?"

"No!" He shouted out in reply before slamming the door shut. We looked at each other as we realised what his answer inevitably meant.

"Oh God, what are we gonna do now?" moaned Leon.

"Replace his drum stool with a commode?" I suggested, unwisely attempting to add some humour to the situation.

"And what's he supposed to do, sit there with his bloody pants round his ankles?" Leon snapped.

"Alright, I wasn't being serious." I mumbled.

"Look, it's no big deal. We'll just go to plan B like I said before. If Wayne needs to get offstage in a hurry, Mac and I can duo a couple of acoustic versions of our numbers until he comes back."

Moments later the toilet door opened and Wayne emerged, patting moisture off his face with paper towels. We all turned to look at him expectantly.

"It's alright, think that might be a one off. I actually feel a little bit better now."

Surprisingly, some colour had returned to his face and he did indeed look a little brighter.

Gina informed him of our plan but he assured us he would make it through the entire show. We retook the stage a short time later feeling collectively a little less anxious than before. By the time Gina came to be bidding the audience goodnight, we could all breathe a sigh of relief; the second set, unlike the contents of our drummer's stomach, had passed calmly.

CHAPTER ELEVEN

Although quite often undervalued, one can never truly understate the remedial benefits of a good night's sleep. Pure and simple, a good solid eight hours of nothing but blissful, uninterrupted slumber can do wonders for both the mind and body. I felt pretty damn chipper, waking and leaping out of bed as I did the next morning. *Carpe Diem*! Seize the day! Yeah, that was me from now on! Not that I had anything out there to go out seizing specifically. My to do list today only actually had two words written on the whole page. Chill out. A shower and shave followed by midday coffee and hot bagels with Gina. A good enough way to start the day for me. Sharing a stage with Wayne and all his bodily ailments last night had completely killed any appetite for a late supper after the gig so I was bloody hungry when I woke up.

Gina nibbled on a croissant. We hadn't spoken much. No need really. Our relationship had reached that point where we saw each other every day, each of which was much like the last, thus bright and bubbly new conversation from either of us was neither expected or demanded. This in turn gave way to many an occasional period of comfortable, mutual bouts of silence.

As good as my rest had been, it had done nothing, it appeared, to improve my memory. It wasn't until we had settled our bill, exited the coffee house and were about to go our separate ways when Gina enquired if I might like to join her later to help shop for a birthday present for her mother in town. Whilst searching for a good enough reason to answer in the negative, I suddenly remembered my plans with Matt. I politely declined Gina's offer.

"Fair enough, whatever." She said indifferently.

"Hey, why don't you come along too? He's bringing his girlfriend so it won't be all man talk. You can always go to the shops for your Mum after can't you?"

"Ugh, a foursome? Don't know if I'm ready for that," she grimaced. "Besides I've only met him once, he was alright, just looks a bit of an unwashed tree hugger to me."

"Oh come on now G, you can't go round saying stuff like that," I scolded, even though I'd thought pretty much the exact same thing myself only the day before.

Some fifty feet or so away, the rear door to the function bar room crashed open and Carlos pushed through carrying three crates full of empty beer bottles. He walked a short way to his left and set them down noisily amongst several others against the back wall. As he stood upright he noticed us watching him and stood staring back at us, brow furrowed, for several long seconds before retreating back into the building.

"So what do you say, you coming?" I turned back to Gina.

"Huh?"

"The pub, are you going to join us?"

"Oh, no I don't think so thanks, Swampy and his other half can have you all to themselves. See you later."

The Dog and Duck was a newly refurbished public house in the middle of town. As part of a nationwide chain it stood bold and large in red brick amongst the older, drabber buildings adjoining it in the street. The coloured signs on the door entrance offered multiple two for one drinks offers and lunchtime meal menus. I took in the interior décor that consisted of dark wood walls, rich carpeting and plush grey velour seating. It still managed, in spite of itself, to exude a nondescript and oddly characterless feel to it. Not that the clientele in here seemed at all bothered of course. I scanned the faces in the room in search of Matt and his girlfriend. Not spotting them I wondered through to a second bar area to the rear of this cavernous pub. They were not anywhere in here either. I decided to get myself one drink and give them the benefit of the doubt that they may just be running late.

I walked over to the beer garden and immediately spotted Matt sat alone at a large wooden table outside. He was leaning back in his seat with his eyes closed and the sun on his face.

"Matt!" I made a drinking gesture with my hand and pointed to his nearly empty pint glass. He gave me a thumbs up and mouthed the word cider. Matt was grinning and smoking a roll up as I approached the table and placed the drinks down.

"Hey, here he is, how's it going man?"

"I'm doing good mate, thanks, how are you?"

"Livin' the dream buddy, livin' the dream."

"Glad to hear it."

We both gulped our pints.

"Cheers! You not on the Guinness then?"

"Ha ha, no I'm not even that fond of the stuff if I'm honest."

"What? An Irishman that doesn't like a drink? Surely no such thing!" He laughed.

"Oh I like a drink, it's just that I'm more of a wine man."

"Ah, connoisseur are we sir?"

"Of the five pounds and under supermarket variety, absolutely!"

"I'll drink to that!"

We cheered.

"So, where's your girlfriend? I thought she was gonna be with you?"

"Oh right, yeah Tam's had to cover for someone over lunch at work, she should be here in about half an hour."

"Ah okay. I take it Tam's short for Tamsin?"

"Nah mate, Tamara," he pronounced the name with a mockingly posh accent. "Don't tell her I told you that though, she comes from a very well to do family, it reminds her of them."

"Right, so she doesn't get on too well with her folks then?"

"They get on okay, I guess, it's just I think they always wanted a little pony riding princess for a daughter, all polished shoes and piano lessons, you know? Tam just ain't that sort of girl." She's in her classic posh girl rebellious stage then, I thought.

"How did you two meet then?"

"Us? It was on a climate change protest march in Brighton. We're both sort of environment activists, she was there with this bloody great long protest banner and no one to hold the other end. Her mate who'd she'd come down with had fainted not long after they'd arrived and had to sit it out. When I saw her, well I wasn't going to leave a damsel in distress was I? So naturally I stepped in and volunteered to help her out," he grinned.

"How very heroic of you." I smiled back.

"Well, not all hero's wear capes Mac. It did help she was quite fit too." He cackled. "It was February then as well so it was bloody freezing, she was just so grateful, she offered to buy me coffee and carrot cake after and that was it, we just hit it off. We've got a flat together now, well, it's hers actually, I think her Dad paid the deposit, but I'm earning now so I pay my way with the bills and that, so it's all good."

"Glad to hear it, mate." We both took a moment to enjoy another gulp from our pint glasses.

"So anyway, who was the hot piece of tail I saw you with the other day?"

"Sorry?"

"The bird in the denim shorts?"

"Oh you saw us? She, that was... that was nobody."

"Oh sure, just gave you a kiss after you gave her directions did she? Right!"

"Alright, alright, her name's Alice. She's my ex-girlfriend." I sighed.

"Your ex-girlfriend. Come down to try and rekindle some fires did she?"

"Kind of, yeah."

"So come on then, what's the story there, how come she's your ex?"

"She was my girlfriend back in London, when I was in the band. Then she started having sex with our drummer."

"Wow, and you were okay with this?"

"Of course I wasn't bloody okay with it! She was screwing him behind my back."

"Oh right, sorry, I thought it was some sort of groupie sharing thing."

"No Matt, believe it or not we weren't quite that close. Anyway the band had folded by this point, basically she got with him and kicked me out on my arse."

"Whoa. Tough break."

"Yeah, you could say that. Ultimately it's why I ended up taking the job here, to get away from London and to get far away from her."

"And she turned up begging for forgiveness, did she?"

"She wanted me to go back to London and move back in with her as if nothing had happened, but no. Let's just say she had one or two ulterior motives to get me back so I sent her packing. She's not a nice person, trust me."

"Sounds like you dodged a bullet there, bud." Matt finished his pint and gestured for me to do the same.

"Same again?"

"Sure, why not." With Matt away at the bar I couldn't help but reflect on my love life. Hearing Matt's happy story with Tam made me slightly jealous. I wanted to be in love again, don't get me wrong I don't want to go back to Alice, I wasn't that desperate. I just wished I had someone who I could talk so lovingly about, my story was getting a little boring.

Matt returned with two full pints and placed them down on the table. He picked up his tobacco pouch and began rolling himself another cigarette. When he'd finished he reached into the pocket of his cargo shorts and took out a silver zippo lighter. I noticed it had some kind of Chinese dragon motif etched into the side of it.

"I'd have done the same thing as you, you know," he said taking a drag and exhaling smoke out the side of his mouth.

"You mean with Alice?"

"Yeah, telling her to get on her bike was the right thing to do."

"Actually it was a train but yeah, I've no regrets there."

"If Tam ever done the dirty on me that would be it, done. Over. I just couldn't handle it." I could tell just the thought of Tam cheating hurt. For the first time I saw a vulnerability in Matt.

"You're pretty sweet on this girl, aren't you?"

Matt reddened a little. "Yeah well, it's just that she's good for me, you know? Keeps me on the straight and narrow."

"How so?"

Matt paused and took a drag of his roll up. "Oh you know, just keeping me going when things get tough. The usual." I could tell he wanted me to press deeper.

"Do things get tough?"

"Nah, nah man…" I stared at him.

"Look, I could tell you something about my past now, but you might not want to hear it."

"Why not?"

"Cause there's a good chance it might make you think less of me."

"We've all got a past, Matt. I'm all ears if you want to share." He sighed and looked around the garden.

"Right, yeah, well, you know I made that stupid joke about

having coke in my bag yesterday?" I nodded. "Well, drugs weren't always something to joke about, not for me."

"Go on."

He took a deep breath before continuing. "A couple of years ago, when I was seventeen, well, there was three of us, mates, I mean. Me, Rob and Charlie. We'd grown up at school together so we were pretty tight. None of us had much of a home life so we used to hang out at each other's houses, just gaming mostly. None of us had jobs either, we were all on this pissy little job seeker's allowance hand out every month so we were skint most of the time. We couldn't afford to go to pubs or clubs or whatever so we used to pool our cash together and send Charlie off to get whatever weed it would buy us, and maybe some cheap tinnies with whatever was left. It wasn't much but at least we could get stoned and have a laugh sometimes, you know? Anyway this one time Charlie comes back and says there was no weed but he's managed to score us something a bit stronger, and did we want to try it?"

"Always starts there, doesn't it?" Matt nodded.

"Anyway, so we had all tried the normal stuff before, you know coke and that. We've all been to festivals we know what to do, but it's not that. It was heroin." His eyes darted at mine to gauge my reaction, I tried not to act surprised. "So yeah, none of us had ever tried it before so we were all a bit nervous and unsure, but Charlie's mate told him what to do so he was ready to show us. We were all nervous but kinda buzzing too, like a weird excitement. In the end we knew it was try this shit or nothing so we said what the hell, fuck it, why not? So we cooked it up and took turns with the needle."

I really had to bite my tongue at this point because not everyone chooses heroin if they can't get weed. It was a little hard to believe. He was right to think I might have thought less of him.

"I'm not gonna lie to you Mac, I've never felt a rush like it… it was a fucking trip. We all said the same thing when we'd come round."

"Wonderful. So you and your mates all became heroin addicts, is that it?"

"No, no, no. We only ever did a little bit at weekends after that, not everyone who does smack becomes an addict you know, same as not everyone who drinks is an alcoholic. They're both drugs."

"I'd say heroin is more addictive than booze though, Matt."

"Oh is it really, Mac? Try telling that to Alcoholics Anonymous."

I sat back in my chair and drank some more beer. I let him have that comment but I definitely did not agree with his twisted logic.

"So anyway, Christmas comes round and Charlie's Nan's ill or something so his Mum and Dad decide to spend it with her. This leaves Charlie home alone for the first time ever on Christmas Eve. Except of course he's not gonna be spending it on his own is he? We can't believe our luck having a whole house to ourselves, so we decide to push the boat out and get ourselves a nice bit of H in and a shit load of cheap booze."

"Merry Christmas!" I retorted.

Matt was beginning to sound like a different guy to the one I had connected with yesterday. He dropped his fag and stubbed it out with his foot on the ground next to him.

"I don't remember much about the evening, it's a bit of a haze. I know we watched a couple of movies, drank and jacked up. I remember coming round and saying I was calling it a night. Rob more or less followed suit at the same time. Charlie said he was gonna stay up a while longer and watch some crap TV. So we left him sat on the sofa with a blanket round him cos the heating had gone off. What me and Rob didn't know was once we'd gone Charlie decided to help himself to a little extra Christmas cheer. All of what was left in the wrap, in fact." He paused for a drink. "I was the first to come down that morning. I opened the living room door and there-there he was. I knew straight away he was dead. The blanket had fallen round his feet and he was slumped backwards with his head back." Matt couldn't look me in the eye. "His lips, they'd turned blue and he had sick down his t-shirt. His arm was dangling over one side and the needle was on the floor."

"Jesus Matt."

"Yeah. I've had nicer surprises on Christmas morning."

"That's shocking."

"Verdict was misadventure, a straightforward overdose. No charges against Rob and me but of course everyone we knew labelled us as junkies."

"That must have been tough to deal with."

"The hardest part was not being allowed to go to Charlie's funeral. His parents wouldn't have it. They blamed us. Guess they needed to blame someone and they saw me and Rob as at least partly responsible. Charlie was our best friend though, we were like brothers. It hurt not being allowed to say goodbye, it really did hurt."

Having heard the full story it was impossible not to feel sympathy for what he had been through at such a young age. As if being the one to find your best friend dead while you had been sleeping upstairs wouldn't have been hard enough, but to have been blamed for it too.

"I'm so sorry to hear all of that mate."

Matt took in a deep breath and sat up straight.

"Well, at least I can now say all that is behind me now. I've got a job I like and a girlfriend who loves me, and that's what I mean when I say she keeps me on the straight and narrow, it's having someone who cares, you know?" He looked up at me. "Life's good now bud, no more mistakes. I have got to stay away from all that shit."

"Good for you Matt."

A tall thin girl with short, black hair wearing leggings and a baggy t-shirt stepped into the beer garden, looked over in our direction and began walking towards our table. Matt turned around and immediately stood to greet her.

"Babe! You made it!" He enthused, leaning in to kiss her.

"Sorry I'm late, I had to cover for that lazy cow Katrina again."

"No worries darl, here have a seat. Tam, this is Mac."

"Hi Tam," I offered my hand out to her.

"Hi Mac, nice to meet you. Matt says I'm supposed to ask for your autograph," she winked, then shook my hand.

"Oh did he? Well, sure that's fine with me, as long as I can sign it on his forehead in black marker pen?"

"Haha be my guest!" laughed Tam.

"I'd better get the drinks in!"

"No, it's my round, I'll get these, what can I get you, Tam?"

"I'll have a gin and lemon please, thanks."

"No worries." I went off to the bar and returned a short while later with a tray of drinks. I decided this had better be my last of the afternoon. Getting hammered and turning up for the show in a few hours' time still half cut would not likely go down too well with the rest of the band.

"Tam's a singer, Mac, did I tell you that?"

"Oh, is that right?"

"Used to be a singer," corrected Tam as she frowned at Matt.

"What sort of music?"

"I sang for a punk band for a while a couple of years ago, that's all. I was dreadful but that was okay cos the rest of the band couldn't really play anyway."

"Tell him what your name was," Matt giggled.

"Name?" I raised my eyebrow at her.

"Well, back in the seventies all the punk singers had to have a punk name didn't they? I liked that idea so I chose my own…"

"And what was yours?" I said, taking a mouthful of beer.

"Eva Brick." Unable to stop myself I spat my drink laughing.

"Oh my god, that is just the best punk name ever!"

"It was a hell of a lot better than my singing anyway!"

I stayed for half an hour or so longer before leaving them to it. I had enjoyed meeting up with them and made the assumption that we would likely do it again soon.

CHAPTER TWELVE

Over the next few weeks I fell back into the same routine of meeting up with Gina in the morning, chilling out in the daytime then doing the shows in the evening. The consistency seemed to clear my head and I began to feel a little happier in my own skin. I was no longer embarrassed about being at Clifton Sands, I was grateful in fact. I had found great friends in Gina and Matt. Seeing them both regularly made me happy. Although, recently Matt hadn't been around much.

Most days here started well, and stayed that way, but on occasions circumstances conspired to bring you down and generally piss on your parade. I was sat outside in the sun with Gina, Leon and Wayne, joking around while drinking coffee when I spotted something in the morning paper.

"Hey, guess what? You'll never guess what day it is."

"Easy, Tuesday." Leon joked.

"Says here it's also International Hug a Musician Day!" I pretended to celebrate.

"Really? Comes around so quickly doesn't it?" said Gina dryly.

"A day to celebrate I'd say, how about it Leon?" I said rising from my chair and extending my arms towards him.

"Oh, go on then," he stood up. "Don't be getting any ideas though, I'm spoken for you know!" He embraced me slightly too tight.

"You look great by the way," I said as we pulled away. "Have you lost weight?"

"Oh, fuck off you cheeky shit, you're not my type in any case, you're far too much of a pretty boy."

"Well I'm sorry to disappoint you. I'm not even going to ask Gina, she'll probably knee me in the balls."

"Count on it."

"Oh God, not another one eh? There won't be any real men left in the world at this rate," Carlos sneered as he walked towards us.

"Well, well Carlos, remind me to add homophobia to the list of reasons you're such an arsehole," Leon rolled his eyes.

"Oh dry your eyes why don't you? Am I wrong to believe a red blooded man belongs in the arms of a red blooded woman, no? Gina knows what I'm talking about don't you baby?"

He squatted down next to her and rubbed her shoulders. She ignored him and continued to keep her eyes on the menu. I noticed she didn't push him away.

"Believe what you like, it takes more than a hairy chest and a fake gold medallion to make a real man in my book," Leon remarked. Carlos was clearly offended. He leaned forward and held up his medallion in front of Leon's face.

"Fake gold huh? Take a closer look, you've never seen one like this before." Leon inspected it.

"Yeah my Nan got one just like it for my Granddad from a gift shop in Torremolinos."

We all smirked, apart from Carlos. He was turning red.

"This," he continued, "is the symbol of the Spanish bull."

"Oh really, so tell me, why do your lot stick spears into them till they're dead in the name of sport then, eh?"

Wayne's turn now.

Carlos shook his head.

"What you speak of is not sport, my friend, oh no. This is an ancient ritual, a dance of death between matador and bull, the conquest of man and beast. The bull dies, yes, but he dies the brave and noble death of a gladiator in the ring."

"Sounds like a load of bullshit to me," I chimed in. Carlos started towards me.

"Carlos? Carlos? There you are, there's people want serving up here, what are you playing at lad, come on." I have never been happier to see Graham in my life.

"You've got a smart mouth Mac, watch it doesn't get you into trouble someday eh?" He picked up some empty glasses and sauntered back to the bar.

"Well, that escalated quickly," I laughed.

"Such an ignorant pig," Leon shook his head. I turned to Gina.

"So how come he didn't get it in the balls then?" I asked.

"Enough of this, I've got to go." She abruptly stood up and left.

"What's her problem?"

"I really don't know." I said as I watched her go. The three of us remained in silence as we watched her leave.

The next few days were frosty between us all but we managed to get through. I was in my room when someone knocked on my door.

"Mac? There's someone in reception asking to see you," Graham called. Not Alice again surely?

"Really? Male or female?"

"Young lad, scruffy bastard an' all."

"Did he say what he wants?"

"Who am I your bloody secretary? How should I know?" He said irritably before marching off.

I made my way to reception, unsure of who it could be waiting for me. A young lad of around eighteen, who did indeed match Graham's description, was standing just inside the door as I entered. He looked up sheepishly as I stopped in front of him,

"Hello, are you looking for me?"

"Are you Mac?"

"Yeah, how can I help?" His eyes shifted nervously.

"Can I have a word, outside?"

"Sure." I held the door open and followed him outside. We turned off the path and walked a short way across the grass before he stopped and turned to face me.

"I'm here about Matt."

"Oh Matt? Well, I haven't really seen him for a while, in fact, I don't even think he's been at work the last few days. Sorry, who are you, a friend of his?"

"Kinda, yeah, I'm Lewis. Look, Matt is in hospital, that's why I'm here, to let you know."

"Hospital? Jesus, is he okay? What was it, was he in some sort of accident?"

The young man paused. Again his eyes shifted around to check no one was within in earshot before answering.

"No, he's okay, nothing like that. He's been stupid, he overdosed."

I was truly stunned.

"Heroin?" Lewis nodded.

"He told me he was done with all that, I can't believe it. When was this?"

"Last night, I think. They've detoxed him and put him on the ward. He wants to know if you'll go see him." I nodded, fixing Lewis with a stare.

"Who gave him this stuff, you?"

"Look, I'm just the bloody messenger boy alright? He's on Audley Ward if you want to go, I couldn't give a toss either way." He spat and walked away.

I seriously considered not going to see Matt. He'd told me heroin was firmly in his past and I'd believed him because he'd seemed genuine. Now he's got himself in such a state that he was in hospital, I didn't know what to believe with him anymore. Maybe he was nothing but a dirty little junkie after all. I'd thought he and I could be friends but, knowing what I knew now did I really need a person like this in my life? What did he want to see me for anyway?

In the end curiosity got the better of me. Once I'd checked out the visiting hours I walked into town and caught the bus to the hospital. After finding Audley Ward impossible to locate, a nurse with brown pigtails finally directed me to it. I wandered through the ward, the smell of disinfectant sharp in the air, looking from side to side at the faces in the beds until I saw him. He was sat up in bed, shirtless and staring straight ahead blankly. I walked over and sat down in the vacant chair next to him.

"Oh, Mac, hey, you came."

"For some reason, yes," I remained stony faced.

"I really appreciate it, bud."

"Yeah, well what are you even doing here you bloody idiot?"

"Nice to see you too!" His attempt at making this all one big joke was not funny to me. Matt lowered his tired eyes. His sunken face looked ghostly white.

"You look like death."

"I know, I feel it an' all."

"Why did you do it Matt? You lied to me."

Matt looked up frowning.

"What did I lie to you about?"

"Oh cut the shit will you? You told me you were done with doing this crap a long time ago?"

"Excuse me," a nurse came over to us.

"Keep your voice and your language down, please, people are trying to rest here."

"Sorry," I apologised.

"I didn't lie, I haven't touched the stuff since that night with Charlie, not till last night that is. It was just a one off, that's all."

"A one off? That is all it takes, Matt. Surely you know that better than anyone. What the hell were you even thinking going back down that stupid road again? I thought that was in the past, I thought you'd got your life shit together now?" I couldn't control my anger, I think I cared about him more than I had realised. "And what's Tam think about it all, she must know you're in here?"

"Alright, alright, enough," he hissed back.

"I fucked up, don't you think I know that? People do make mistakes you know Mr Righteous. I thought you'd be the one person who might actually listen and understand."

I'd heard enough already. I stood up to leave.

"The only mistake you're making is fucking up all the good things you have in your life now, and all to get your kicks sticking a needle in your arm. Good luck mate, I hope you get it sorted out." I turned to go.

"Tam, Tam doesn't know. She doesn't know because she ended things with me, okay." He said miserably.

I stopped and turned back to him. It was plain to see he was on the verge of tears. With a sigh I stepped back and retook my seat. I gave him a moment to compose himself.

"What happened?"

"I don't know man," he said quietly. "She sat me down last week, told me she wasn't happy anymore, that my moving in had been much too soon and now she just felt trapped and tied down. I tried to talk her out of it, I practically begged; sad really. I couldn't persuade her though, she told me she wanted me to move out." His voice cracked.

In that moment, I knew exactly why Matt had wanted to talk to me and why he thought I would be the one to understand. I could empathise perfectly. I tried to find words of solace and comfort for him but my own, all too recent experience made it difficult. There isn't really anything you can say to make it hurt any less.

"I suggested that we could go on a break for a few weeks, give her some time on her own, a bit of head space, you know?

I was willing to do that to save the relationship but she said she didn't need any more time to think about it." Tears welled up in his eyes. He wiped them away. "So I'm living at Mum and Dad's again, I just feel like my whole life's in reverse, Mac. Right back to square one again."

"I know mate, but you've just got to hang in there, give it some time, things will get better."

"Ever since I moved back home I've been low, really, really low. I could hardly get out of bed even, just couldn't face the day. It got to Saturday night and I thought, screw it, I'll go to the pub, on my own but only to get fucking hammered and crawl back to my hole. Well, I'd been there a couple of hours and I was certainly well on the way, when in comes Lewis and his mate Fez, Lewis was the one who came to see you."

"Yes, I've had the pleasure."

"Yeah, well I knew him but not his mate Fez; I'd heard his name before though. He's a dealer about town. I think Charlie might have known him."

"So didn't you just want to smack him in the face?"

"Maybe I would have before, instead they offered me some. I know you think I'm weak, stupid, dirty, disgusting, whatever but I needed to feel good so badly, something to take all the pain away, for all this shit and misery to just disappear, just for a while. So we went to the park and jacked up but my body wasn't used to it. That's what happens when you reuse after a long time without it, your system can't take the hit like it could when you were doing the shit regular. That's what happened to me last night, which is why I'm here, as you already know."

"Did they leave you on your own?"

"Nah, Lewis called the ambulance but they both legged it when it turned up."

I guess they were decent enough to call for an ambulance. To break the intensity of the conversation I took a time out to go and get us a coffee each. I needed a moment to gather my thoughts on the situation. I returned to the seat by the bed a short while later.

"Do you want me to grab you anything for while you're in here? Maybe a book or something to take your mind off of stuff."

Matt shook his head without looking up. He looked defeated and drained. It was almost time for me to get the bus back to the camp.

"When are they letting you go home?"

"Whenever they sign me off, probably in the morning sometime. My folks will pick me up."

"Promise me you will call me as soon as you get out. We'll get together. A coffee or a beer, a walk on the beach, whatever you like, just a hang out and chat, yeah? Anytime you feel like it, okay?"

"I promise." Matt lifted his head and finally looked me in the eye.

"Thanks for being a friend, Mac."

Slightly taken back by this unexpected reply, I merely nodded and patted him on the shoulder.

CHAPTER THIRTEEN

On the bus journey back and for the rest of the evening I couldn't get Matt out of my head. As much as I cared about what he had gone through, I just couldn't understand why he had turned back to drugs. He'd had a tough start to his adult life that was for sure, but he certainly wasn't the first teenager to experience alienation and poverty through unemployment, or to dabble in dangerous drugs for that matter. He might not be happy where he was now but being home with his Mum and Dad meant he did at least have a support system in place. I know to have Tam break up with him and ask him to move out was devastating for him, of course, I understood and sympathised. Yet, you had to take a look at the bigger picture, Matt was only nineteen. He had his whole life in front of him. Tam might just be his first love and the first to break his heart but the ups and downs of relationships were part of life, not just for him but for us all. Whatever doesn't kill you makes you stronger and I knew in my heart that, despite what I'd seen earlier that Matt had the strength of character to get through this, to pick himself up and get over Tam and get over this drugs blip. Anyway, as long as we kept in touch I could keep an eye on him.

It was Gina's birthday at the end of the week and I considered asking Matt if he wanted to join us for the night down the pub we'd arranged to celebrate. Thinking about it though Gina hadn't exactly seemed that keen on him before. Nor had she been particularly complimentary about him either but I knew

Gina, and I knew deep down she had a caring side.

"Are you having a fucking laugh? Not only are you asking me if I want a member of the great unwashed joining me on my birthday evening but now you're doubling that up by telling me he's a bloody heroin addict too."

"Right, look, first of all he's not an addict, at least I don't think he is, it's like I told you, he used to do it now and again in the past. He's only took it again this once, although I admit stupidly, because he's just broken up with his girlfriend, he's badly upset and that's why he ended up in hospital. Come on Gina, cut him some slack, he's had a tough time in the last few years and after all we all know what it feels like getting dumped."

"Yeah but most of us don't stick a needle in our arm and get smacked off our tits to get over it."

"No. No, of course we don't, but all of us have a past and I honestly feel this overdose thing really scared the shit out of him. I think he's learned his lesson this time, I really do."

"Why do you care so much anyway? Thought you hardly knew him."

"I don't really know him that well, no, it's true but we've shared some stuff alright? For some reason he looks up to me, he listens to me."

"Why? Cos you were a pop star for five minutes?" I refused to rise to her childishness.

"Because he needs a half decent friend right now that's why, someone to give him a bit of their time, maybe even invite them out to a social function of some sort?"

Gina sighed and rolled her eyes.

"Oh alright, whatever. If you want to bring him fine, he can be your plus one. Maybe you can buy him some deodorant or subtly spray him with air freshener or something before you come."

"You, Gina, are an angel, thank you. Heaven must be missing one I swear because you're right here among us spreading your celestial love and kindness." Gina gave me a sarcastic smile while raising her hand and mimicking the spraying motion of a bottle with her finger, before offering me her middle one.

"May Mother Mary bless you," I blew her a kiss.

As it happened I needn't have bothered persuading Gina as Matt never showed up for work at the camp in the days leading up to her birthday night. Maybe it was a good sign, perhaps he was feeling stronger and more positive in himself and didn't feel the need to lean on someone. So why then wasn't he turning up for work? Maybe his folks felt he needed more time at home with them or something, how should I know? I simply didn't know the guy well enough to second guess his movements, that was the truth of the matter. I guess we'd meet and talk sooner or later, I just thought it would have been nice to have got him out with us amongst some friendly faces who would look out for him.

The band only got one Saturday night off every four weeks so this event was to be made the most of. On our nights off, Graham always booked a comedy night featuring live stand-up routines from the circuit comedians. I was glad to not be witness to the evening of 'nonstop laughter and mirth'.

As evening came, I showered and dressed in the same outfit I used to favour when going onstage with Rebel Shout. Black slim-fit, short-sleeved shirt and skinny black jeans, I stared into my small bathroom mirror as I put the finishing touches to the gel in my hair. I sprayed some inexpensive aftershave liberally around my neck and I was done. I looked good. I was feeling good. I smelled great. I was ready to party. I met up with Gina, Leon and Wayne at the camp entrance to share a taxi into town. If I'd thought I looked pretty good then Gina was looking absolutely knockout in a short, black designer dress and matching black stilettos. The less said about Leon and Wayne's dress sense the better. We had opted to push the boat out and head to some of the cooler bars Brighton had to offer. I was looking forward to it. Despite inviting Elena, Chloe and a few other staff members at the camp, everyone it seemed was occupied or busy so it was going to be just the four of us. Nobody really minded this as it felt more like a band night out this way.

"I can't believe I'm twenty-five," said Gina.

"What about us?" replied Leon gesturing to Wayne and himself. "We're closer to double that! Oh to be twenty-five again, eh babe?"

Wayne sighed and nodded in reply.

"Sorry, it just feels like that's my youth gone, from here on I'm pushing thirty," she moaned.

"Well console yourself by taking a look at yourself in the mirror love because you look totally fabulous my darling."

"I'll second that," I added looking over my shoulder to give her a wink.

"Ah thanks boys, you all look gorgeous too. Not sure I'll

look quite as pretty when I'm puking up in the toilet later but I won't worry about that now."

The taxi dropped us off and we proceeded to hit Brighton's most cosmopolitan strip of packed bars. Over the next few hours we drank wine and cocktails, laughed and had the best damn night ever, even sharing a tray of garish coloured, vile shots. That is to say, Gina and I did, the boys abstained from this alcoholic insanity on the grounds that hangovers at their age took days to get over. Perhaps it was the influx of alcohol working its influence at this point but, as much as I had come to accept Gina as a firm friend of the platonic kind, it was hard not to find her attractive on such an occasion as this. She looked sexy as hell. The little devil on my shoulder was whispering in my ear not to bother trying. I certainly wasn't the only man this evening, men were literally mesmerised by her every time we walked into a new bar.

Acutely aware that I would probably be rejected, I decided the best to do was to keep my amorous notions in check. As Gina and I downed the last of the shots, wincing at the sharpness of the taste, Leon appeared in front of us and placed a hand on the shoulder of each of us.

"If it's alright with you kids, it's been a blast but we'd like to call it a night and get a cab back to Edmouth now, is that okay?"

"Yeah, sure. Fine with me. G?" I said, looking across at her as she gazed down at her phone. She paused before looking up with a slightly glazed smile.

"Sure, who fancies one last night cap in the Dog and Duck to finish the night off?" She asked.

"No, you're alright Gina love, I hear my bed calling me." Wayne declined.

"Me too," added Leon.

"I'm up for it, let's do it."

Half an hour later, the cab finally pulled up outside The Dog and Duck. Once inside, we found it quieter than expected, possibly because the younger generation had already left for the nightclubs. I wasn't bothered, I was happy to be spending the remainder of the evening with Gina to myself. We reached the bar.

"What's your poison then, birthday girl?"

"Ooh, Prosecco please, Mac."

"Coming up." I caught the eye of the barman and ordered Gina her drink along with a bottle of lager for myself. I took a casual look round at the thirty something other punters in the room. I locked eyes with a familiar face. Standing in front of the cigarette machine was Lewis. Upon clocking me, he quickly purchased his pouch of tobacco and disappeared through into the other bar. I wondered if he'd heard from Matt. He didn't seem overly keen to come over for a chat but I wasn't going to let that stop me. The barman brought the two drinks and placed them on the bar in front of me. I paid him and turned to Gina who hadn't looked up from her phone.

"Won't be a sec, just going to say hi to someone."

"Kay," she said absently.

I strolled across the room and through into the other bar. There was even fewer people in here, a handful of bar flies, a couple of guys on a fruit machine, various small groups sat at tables. No sign of Lewis. I noticed the door at the rear of the room was slightly ajar. I crossed the room and opened it, peered out into the dimly lit area of table benches where I had sat before with Matt. It was deserted. He was gone. With one last look I stepped back inside and closed the door. With that I walked back through into the other room to Gina. The sight that greeted me at the bar stopped me stone dead in my tracks. My mouth dropped open. Gina was smiling and laughing in conversation with the man sat on the barstool, my barstool, next to her. It was Carlos. What the hell? What the fuck was he doing sat there? Gina noticed me mid laugh and waved me over, giving me a 'look who's here' face. I forced a smile back and walked over to them trying my best to appear unruffled.

"Guess who dropped by?" grinned Gina girlishly. I grinned back and nodded. I didn't have to guess did I? The fat tosser was sat right in front of me, in my bloody seat.

"Hey, Carlos, good to see you," I lied.

Carlos took his eyes off Gina's legs long enough to turn and give me a brief upwards nod in silent acknowledgment.

"Hey look," I turned to Gina, "I've just got to go and return a missed call from my Mum."

"Your Mum? Really? It's awfully late, I hope everything's okay?"

"Oh yeah, yeah, I'm sure it's fine, back in a bit."

No way I was going to pull up a chair now and play gooseberry to those two. Christ, what a shit end to a great night. I pulled across the nearest stool and sat down for some reason in front of the fruit machine. I'd never really played one before and didn't have a clue what I was doing but I needed distraction. The machine flashed a multitude of migraine-inducing coloured lights in rapid sequence. I took a pound coin out of my pocket and pushed it into the coin slot. A series of loud bleeping noises and a flashing message displayed on the screen informed me I was now entitled to five plays. Irritably I smacked down on the go button. The four wheels bearing fruit icons began to spin at high speed before coming to a juddering halt one after another.

Thunk! Thunk! Thunk! Thunk!

I hit the stupid button again. I couldn't believe this was how a perfect evening was ending.

Thunk! Thunk! Thunk! Thunk!

Another hit to the button. How could she be so happy to sit chatting with that meathead?

Thunk! Thunk! Thunk! Thunk!

I smacked down on the button again, harder this time. He wasn't even invited, he had no right gate crashing now.

Thunk! Thunk! Thunk! Thunk!

An ear splitting siren noise suddenly erupted. I looked around the room, convinced the fire alarm must have gone off. Then I realised it was coming from the fruit machine right in front of me. I looked at the screen. All that was flashing now were the words:

ONE HUNDRED POUND JACKPOT WINNER!!!!!

The four stationary wheels now shared an identical pound sign icon. Oh my God. Pound coins suddenly began to cascade and clatter down noisily into the coin tray at the bottom. I looked up to see most of the drinkers in the room looking across in my direction, many of them smiling and nodding in congratulation. I started to laugh in disbelief as I scooped up the coins and filled my pockets with them. Well, well, this was certainly turning out to be a night of twists and turns. A shadow fell across my line of vision as I gathered up the last of the money.

"Are you taking the fucking piss or what?"

I looked up, still with a fixed grin on my face, to see two men standing over me.

"Sorry?"

"You think we're gonna stand for being hustled?" The other growled.

"Hustled?"

"Me and him have put the best part of twenty quid each into that machine, we step away to get a pint at the bar and you come and take our jackpot. That money's ours."

I stood up straight to face them.

"Oh no, no, you've got it all wrong boys. Luck of the Irish, that's all it is. Tell you what, how about I buy you both another drink instead for the sake of good will, eh?"

"You cheeky fucker!" His mate quickly placed a restraining hand on his arm.

"Gaz, not 'ere." I took a couple of steps back as the pair of them continued to glare angrily at me.

"Suit yourselves." I turned towards the bar. When I got there the barmaid was smiling at me.

"Looks like someone got lucky tonight."

Yes, though perhaps not in the way I'd anticipated.

"Could I change this lot for notes please?"

I emptied my pockets.

"Course you can, my love."

I bought her a drink for her trouble then headed to the men's room. I guessed I'd better be getting back to Gina and her unwanted guest about now. At least I'd do so richer in wealth if not in enthusiasm.

The door crashed open as I stood alone at the sink washing my hands. My heart sunk as I looked up to see my new fruit machine friends lunging towards me. Oh dear. This did not look good.

"Right you, hand it over. Now."

"Sorry lads, drink offer's expired." I attempted to push past them. With the fluency and grace of a man who'd likely done this a few times before, one of them swung me backwards with one arm, slammed me against the wall then drove his fist into my ribs. Pain erupted in my midriff as the air was violently forced out of my lungs, I doubled over only for his partner in crime to join in the assault by kneeing me hard in the side of the head. I feared for just how bad this may get. Two against one always ends badly. A deep voice from the doorway brought a halt in proceedings.

"What's going on here, boys?" All three of us looked up, me the last and slowest, my vision blurred as I tried to focus. Carlos stood in the doorway.

"It's this paddy prick Carlos, he's been giving us some lip, and he owes us, so we're teaching him a…"

"He's with me." Suddenly I was free from grappling hands.

"With you? Shit, Carlos, sorry, we didn't know."

Tension crackled in the air as Carlos simply stared at both men expressionless before bellowing.

"Get out of here." With the demeanour of two chastised school boys being dismissed by their teacher, the two thugs obeyed and exited without further question. Carlos looked at me as I straightened, gasping a little as the air returned to my body.

"Okay?"

"Yeah… thanks."

Without another word he turned and left. By the time I'd gathered myself and walked back through to the other bar, Gina was sat on her own again.

"There you are, I was about to come looking for you."

"Where's Carlos?"

"Literally just left, he had to get back. Are you okay? Why are you holding your ribs?" I told her everything.

"Are you going to call the police?"

"Nah, they only got a couple of hits in before Carlos stopped them, no bones broken. Besides he obviously knows them, doesn't he?"

"Mmm, he's had a few businesses in Edmouth over the years, maybe they used to work for him? Either way looks like you owe him one."

"Guess it does." This would take some wrapping my head around. I loathed this man, now I found myself firmly indebted to him.

"Shall we make a move?" suggested Gina.

"Yeah, let's."

"How was your Mum by the way?"

"My Mum? Oh my Mum, yeah, went straight to answerphone, she must have already gone to bed after all."

"Oh right."

CHAPTER FOURTEEN

The next morning, I assessed my aches and bruises. I was surprised just how much my body didn't hurt. My head, however, was a different story. The combination of taking a knee into my right temple and an entire evening of alcohol consumption had rendered me in urgent need of some pain killers. Steering clear of The Clifton's 'double the price of anywhere else' mini shopping centre, I decided to walk up to the promenade and into town to find a pharmacy.

The fresh air and exercise would no doubt provide a natural aid to kick start my road to recovery too.

When I returned to the camp, having taken a good long walk along the beach on the way back, I was feeling clear-headed. As I neared my chalet, Gina was coming up the path also.

"Mac, I was just coming to see you."

"Good morning, my lovely, I'm just back from a little seaside stroll to clear the cobwebs, how are you? How's your head this morning?" I asked cheerfully, but Gina wasn't smiling.

"Do you want to sit down somewhere?"

She had something on her mind. I agreed and we walked back to my chalet. Once inside she sighed, appearing nervous.

"I'm afraid I've got bad news."

"Bad news? Carlos wants some payment for being my bodyguard or something?"

"No Mac. It's something else."

I don't think we had ever had a conversation without Gina

being slightly sarcastic. It must be serious.

"Go on then spit it out."

"It's your friend Matt, apparently he overdosed again." A cold air fell on the room.

"Oh for Christ's sake no, not again. That bloody idiot, fuck, I am so pissed off at him. I suppose he's back in hospital again now, is he? Well, I'll tell you what, maybe some of his arsehole drug dealer buddies can go visit him instead of me this time if he wants a bloody shoulder to cry on."

I knew something was wrong when I didn't hear from him. Why did I ignore my instinct.

"Mac, you don't understand. He's not in hospital again, no he… he's dead. He overdosed and he died. I'm so sorry."

I felt the colour drain from my face as I stared at Gina in stunned disbelief.

"Dead? Where did you hear this?"

"I was in the office earlier when Graham took the call," she answered softly. "We thought it might be easier if I came over to tell you."

"I can't believe it." Actually the sad thing was, I could.

"Come on, let's get out of here for a bit, maybe go get a coffee." I nodded silently.

We made our way in silence, I felt like everyone around me had been put on mute.

"Who found him?"

"His Mum, Graham said."

"What a selfish…"

"Yeah, must have been horrible for her," Gina sympathised.

That was an understatement. My throat felt tight.

"I should have gone round to see him. I had all the time in the world but I just didn't bother." Gina immediately put her drink down.

"Right, now then, McIntyre, you listen to me. This is in no way your fault, do you hear me? It's nobody's. How much do you think his Mum and Dad are hurting right now and no doubt blaming themselves, but it's not their fault either. No matter how much you care about someone you can't monitor them twenty four seven, Mac. If Matt wanted to do this he was going to do it and no one could have stopped him".

"'I could have done more though, I could've tried harder to reach out to him."

"No Mac, he had your number and he knew you were there for him, you made that clear. You weren't the reason he was hurting and so you weren't the solution either."

"So what are you saying? That this is on his ex for dumping him?"

"No, of course I'm not saying that, you can't date someone on the premise that they'll top themselves if you dump them. If this was his way of blocking out the pain to get over her then, well, even if this was accidental he knew only too well the risk he was taking."

"Or maybe he just didn't care."

"Either way, this isn't on you okay?" I had never seen this side to her, she comforted me and kept me going.

The days leading up to Matt's funeral passed in something of a daze. Although I had only known him fleetingly, the sudden impact of his death had left me dulled and introspectively sombre. It didn't help that no one else within the camp really knew him at all, so no one could really talk to me about him. Most avoided trying to, understandably.

Wayne handed me a local newspaper that had a short write up on his passing but I couldn't bring myself to read it. A few lines stating a heroin user had died of an overdose would only be written to leave the reader with little or no sympathy. Dance with the devil and your day will come to pass. Good riddance some would say. Graham had asked if I would attend the funeral as a representative of Clifton Sands. I told him this was fine as I had intended to go anyway.

When the day came around, I awoke with a unsteady feeling I had never experienced before. A concoction of sadness, anger, loneliness and regret. I made my way into the grounds of the crematorium. The sun shone brightly in a cloudless blue sky. Inside, the place was filling up. I hung back until everyone had entered before approaching the door myself. As I walked through into the main room I saw a party of about thirty people, Matt's family and relatives, most of them with their backs to me as they arrange themselves in the rows of seats to the left and the right. A light wooden coffin with a garland of white flowers lay centrally ahead of them. An attendee on my right handed me a cream coloured order of service. I thanked him and took a seat towards the back on my own.

The cover read:

A Celebration of the Life of Matthew Daley

Sat alone at the back, I noticed Elena. I was surprised to see her and we exchanged solemn smiles before turning around as the service started. When it was over, I waited outside and kept a respectful distance from the other mourners knowing that nobody would know who I was.

"Hi, Mr Mac."

"Hi Elena, sorry, I didn't know you were coming." She nodded.

"I wanted to come, he used to come over and talk with me sometimes outside when he takes a cigarette break, he always joke and make me laugh, is so very sad."

"Yeah I know, he was a good guy."

The wake was held in a pleasant tearoom across the road, so Elena and I walked over to join his family members. The room was lifeless, a long white table waited at the back. It was filled with clingfilm covered plates containing sandwiches, sausage rolls, quiches and cakes. I got a cup of tea for Elena and I, we sipped these as we looked around the room, stood slightly to the side, away from everyone. I turned my head as a small woman approached me.

"Hello, are you… Mark?"

"Hi, I'm Mac."

"Oh yes, it's Mac, of course that's it. Matthew said he'd made a friend at the holiday camp, I wondered if it was you. I'm Karen, Matthew's mum."

"Nice to meet you, I'm so sorry for your loss, Mrs Daley. This is Elena, we both knew Matt, she works at the camp too."

"Hello, I am sorry for you and your family," Elena stepped

forward, tears immediately beginning to well up in her eyes.

"Oh bless you." Karen reached out to take Elena's hands. "Thank you both, it has been a difficult time for everyone I'm sure you can understand. I admit I'm still finding it very hard to come to terms with I'm afraid. He had his whole life out there ahead of him didn't he? We knew he had his demons of course, we just hoped he'd get through this dark time, but it wasn't to be."

"He is at peace with God now." Elena comforted her with an earnest innocence. A younger woman called her name and with that Mrs Daley urged us to help ourselves to further refreshments from the buffet table and politely excused herself.

We left the wake around half an hour later. Elena offered me a lift the short distance back to camp in her tiny, battered white Fiat but I declined. I wanted to walk instead, to gather my thoughts. I wondered what Tam was doing today, did she even know it was his funeral?

Those in grief often feel the need to seek blame for their loss. In my mind, Tam was in no way responsible or to blame for Matt's demise. A sad state of affairs if anyone had thrown the blame on her though. She must be torn to pieces by what has happened, absolutely devastated. Whatever her reasons, she was entitled to make her choice. For my part, I would forever feel that I could've done more. Perhaps making one call or one visit might have changed things, but that is something I will have to live with.

In the days that followed, life went on at Clifton Sands holiday camp. This was never more accentuated than Graham storming into the function room one afternoon as we sat idly passing the time chatting. He practically had steam coming out of his ears.

"You will not believe the bloody morning I have had, honestly," he announced. "Some dirty little bleeder has only gone and shat themselves in the kiddies' end of the main pool. I've had to close it for the rest of the day and have the whole bloody thing chemically cleaned. Closed all day! People are up in arms already! What the hell else do they expect me to do? It's the bloody parents' fault, why don't they put a nappy on it or shove a cork up the little bugger's arse or summit before they take their sodding brats into the pool? Bloody save me a load of grief and heartache I tell you." He fumed, before stomping off in the direction of the kitchen.

"I take it Graham and Joyce have a childless marriage?" I asked.

"I believe so, how did you guess?" answered Leon.

"Just a hunch."

Moments later Gina entered the room and headed straight to the bar, she too seemed to have a face like thunder.

"She doesn't look too happy either."

"Must be something in the water."

"Don't tell Graham that," I joked.

Gina came over from the bar, drink in hand, and wordlessly pulled up a chair at our table. She looked utterly beside herself over something.

"You alright there, love?" asked Wayne with concern.

"No, Wayne, I'm not. I'm not in the least bit alright actually."

"What is it G? You look white as a sheet."

Gina sat staring straight ahead at the table in front of her, frowning. After a moment she stood straight up, her chair scraping on the floor as she pushed it backwards. She reached into the back pocket of her black skinny jeans and pulled out a white envelope. She sat back down again and tossed it into the centre of the table.

"I've been invited to a wedding."

"Your sister?" I asked. Gina raised her head but didn't reply. She didn't have to. She looked like she might either scream or cry. Or possibly both.

"Yes," she admitted finally. "My sister and my ex-boyfriend are getting hitched, isn't it wonderful? And just to rub my nose deeper in the shit they're inviting me to come along and witness the whole thing!"

The table fell silent with none of us able to think of anything to say.

"So, do you think you'll go?"

Never have I ever seen anyone regret asking something as quick as Wayne did with this one. Gina stood up, picked her brandy glass up and drained the contents in one swallow. She banged the empty glass back down on the table, we all flinched.

"No Wayne, I don't suppose I will. That is unless I can get hold of an AK47 beforehand."

She stormed out.

"Well, tonight is going to be fun."

CHAPTER FIFTEEN

Our performance that evening was a somewhat edgier affair than usual. This was largely due to Gina's mood as she took the stage. Normally she dealt with the over amorous call outs from drunken males with a range of put downs. This inebriated catcalling was almost an inevitable occurrence such is the coupling of men and alcohol. Embarrassing if you ask me. In fairness to Gina, despite the odd spiky comment, she kept her inner turmoil at bay throughout the show. The three of us in the group could sense the darkness in her mood but the audience, as usual, were none the wiser. However, with just three songs remaining on the set list, I began to breathe a little easier.

Then one pissed up little prat stepped forward and lit the blue touch paper. As Gina was introducing the next song a lad in baggy jeans and a reversed baseball cap walked boldly to the front of the stage, placed his pint glass down and leaned up to her, "Nice dress love, would look better on my bedroom floor!" He winked. His two mates, who were dressed practically the same, guffawed loudly from a table behind him. He turned round to acknowledge their approval with a slobbery grin. When he turned back, Gina was smiling sweetly down at him.

"The only thing your Mum finds on your bedroom floor, sonny, is used tissues," she said, directly into the mic.

Oh shit.

The young man's grin evaporated, his face reddening in

anger and embarrassment as he found most of the room now laughing at him.

"You... you cheeky bitch, you..." The words stuck in the young man's throat, his eyes suddenly bulged in apparent pain and his mouth dropped open. I looked down to see Gina's stilettoed right foot standing on the hapless youth's hand. With her other foot she casually kicked over his pint glass onto him. I looked up to get the attention of security but they were already bumbling over. He was escorted out of the bar, holding his hand in pain and his friends running behind. Gina spoke into the microphone again.

"Aw bless him, his mummy must be here to pick him up, night, night!"

"Psycho!" He screamed before finally being bundled out of the exit door.

"That's it, let's call it a night."

Thank you, Leon!

We unplugged our instruments and awkwardly made our way off the stage to the side. Gina led the way and was the first to be confronted by a furious Graham waiting in the wings.

"What the hell was that all about Gina? This is supposed to be a respectable, family holiday camp, not some dive bar, bloody roadhouse! You can't go treating the clientele like that."

"Well maybe you need a better class of clientele then," she snapped.

"Look, it's your job to sing, so ignore them and just bloody well sing next time, alright?" he retorted.

"Tell you what, Graham, why don't you sing instead? You'd

make a great Queen tribute." She threw the mic at him and walked out.

"What does she mean Queen tribute? I can't bloody sing can I? Who does she think she is talking to me like that? Anyway I don't look anything like Franny Mercury do I?"

"No, Graham," sighed Leon, "you don't."

"Listen, she's your responsibility while she's in this band, you lot need to keep her in line. Sort her out!"

"She's just got a lot on her mind at the moment," I defended her. "I'll go talk to her."

I spotted Gina walking away further up the pathway. She was carrying her stilettos in her hand and walking in bare feet.

"G! Hey, wait up!" I called after her. Gina looked round, saw it was me, rolled her eyes and reluctantly paused to wait for me.

"Whatever it is you want to say Mac, you'd better not be about to start lecturing."

She set off pacing again, I struggled to keep up with her.

"Just checkin' my soul sister's chillin' down, that's all," I said trying to keep it light but Gina wasn't playing.

"I'm fine."

"Look, you know I am your friend. We can talk about it."

"I don't want to. Sorry, was I not making that obvious enough?"

We reached her chalet and stopped outside.

"Listen Mac, I appreciate your concern, really I do, but if I want a shoulder to cry on I'll ask for it, alright? Now, none of this is your doing, it's not your fault and, frankly it's none of your business, so if you don't mind, it's been a long day."

"Sure, no problem, sorry."

"Goodnight, Mac." She closed her door before I could even reply.

I stood staring at the closed door for a few minutes. Back at my chalet, I took a hot shower and made myself a cup of black coffee. Graham had been right, of course, as manager to say that such a scene should never have taken place in what was expected to be a family friendly environment. No doubt he will have to respond to complaints tomorrow, but Gina had been provoked into retaliation by a drunken dickhead. I was about to turn in for the night when there was a knock on my door. I picked up my phone and checked the time. It was ten to midnight. For a moment I thought it must be Graham, maybe wanting to know what Gina had said, please God no, I think we'd all had enough confrontation with Graham for one night already. Wearily I unlocked and opened the door only slightly and peered out. It was Gina.

"Hello."

"Hi."

"Sorry I was an arsehole earlier."

"No, you weren't, it's fine."

"Well, I was. You were trying to be nice and I was just plain, bloody rude."

"It's okay, really. You were just a bit upset that's all, and understandably so."

Gina brought her hands round from behind her back and held up a bottle of red wine in one and a couple of glasses in the other.

"Peace offering?"

"Oh, okay…" I smiled.

"Unless you were going to bed, sorry, it is rather late I know."

"No, no, don't be silly, of course not," I lied. "Come on in."

"No," she shook her head. "It's a lovely night, let's go down and sit on the beach, don't worry, I won't keep you out all night."

"Why Mrs Robinson, are you trying to seduce me?" I grinned.

"What? Who the hell is Mrs Robinson?" She frowned.

"Not seen *The Graduate* then?"

She shook her head blankly.

"I'll just get my jacket."

We made our way down the pathway to the beach, I sensed a slight sway in the way Gina walked and guessed she may already be one or two drinks ahead of me. We walked further up until we reached an area of dunes where Gina decided she wanted to sit. It was the perfect spot, with the tide far out in front of us and the sand still warm beneath our feet. The rise of the dune was just enough to keep out the faintest chill from the late night ocean breeze. Apart from a lone dog walker in the distance, the beach was all ours. I laid down my jacket on the sand next to me for Gina to sit on. She handed me the bottle and two glasses. We sat in silence for a moment, listening to the waves breaking on the shore ahead in complete moonlit ambience. I opened the bottle and carefully poured a glass for each of us.

"Had you ever been to Edmouth before you came to Clifton?" she asked, taking the glass.

"Me? No, I've barely been out of London since we moved to be honest. Once I got on the band circuit it was pretty full on, not something you really get a chance to take much of a holiday from."

"What about when you were a kid? Did you go to the coast much then?"

"No, we were never really a seaside holiday family, I don't know why. They preferred long walks in the countryside. Back in Ireland we'd always get a caravan for a week somewhere rural with hills and forests, right out in the sticks, you know? Or sometimes camping, just going out fishing or hiking, sit around a campfire in the evenings. I loved it, the great outdoors. I never got bored."

"Sounds idyllic. I've never been to Ireland."

"You should go, the Southern parts are beautiful, you can really lose yourself there."

"Do you miss it?"

"Sure, sometimes. We used to go back every year when I was young to visit relatives, I sort of forgot about it when I grew up, there was just so much going on in London, all that bright lights, big city shit, music became the big thing in my world and it felt like I was in the perfect place for it, life really took off for me. Well, at least I thought it had." I said trailing off.

Gina reached across and lightly patted my hand sympathetically. She knew the rest.

"How about you? Ever been here before?"

Gina nodded.

"Yeah, Mum and Dad used to bring us here most summers, back when me and Lucy were little kids."

"At Clifton Sands?"

"Oh God no, Dad considered holiday camps beneath us. He was strictly a Bed and Breakfast man, he wouldn't have his family stay in anything that wasn't made of brick and mortar. It was an easy holiday for Mum and Dad, at that age me and Lucy didn't want for anything else but to spend all day running around on the beach, building sandcastles and eating ice creams in the sun. If it was raining Dad would take us to the arcades while Mum went off to look round the shops, he'd give us each one of those plastic tubs full of two pence pieces to shovel in the machines. He had to keep lifting us up cos we weren't tall enough to reach the coin slots. Sometimes we'd just stay on the beach in the rain and paddle in the sea, we didn't care, we just loved being here." I watched Gina's moonlit face as she smiled wistfully to herself at the memory.

"That sounds really lovely." Gina turned her head to look at me.

"It was. Those were honestly the purist, happiest days of my entire childhood, just joyous and innocent…"

It was Gina's turn to tail off, she turned her head back again, her eyes dropped to the sand in front of her. Not for the first time I sensed a sadness overcome her.

She picked up her wine and finished her glass.

"Never mind." She handed me her glass for a refill. I finished off the bottle between us.

"Is that why you took the singing job at the Clifton? To be back here?"

"Yes. I needed to escape somewhere, to just get away. When

I saw this job come up at the agency I knew straight away this was the place I wanted to come. I needed to be somewhere that held fond memories. A happy place."

"When did you last holiday here?"

"Oh we stopped coming when I was still only little, Mum decided she wanted to go abroad for our holidays instead so we started going on package holidays to Greece or Spain every year, it was nice but somehow it was never the same as coming here, some of the magic was lost, every hotel resort abroad we stayed in looked exactly the same you know? All identical palm trees and swimming pools. I honestly think Dad would have preferred to stay and keep coming here, so would I, but Mum usually got her way so things changed." She shrugged her shoulders. "Lucy was happy, she was always Mum's favourite so she always sided with her."

"Were you always a Daddy's girl then?" I teased. She paused before answering.

"Yeah."

"How was your relationship with your mum?" I cringed at myself for sounding like her analyst.

"Strained for the best part," she replied with a sigh. "Mum always had a certain vanity about her, she could be very aloof with all of us, including Dad. It's something I picked up on and disliked about her from an early age, sometimes she could just be not very nice towards us I suppose, like sometimes we bored her. It had the opposite effect on Lucy, it seemed to inspire an awe of Mum in her, a constant need to feel acceptance from her. It was all she wanted. She idolised that bloody woman, still does. Dad was the one I looked up to. He held all the warmth and kindness she lacked, I know parents aren't supposed to have favourites but I knew without a doubt I was his, the same as Lucy was Mum's. We shared laughs and stories together as if they were secrets from everyone else, I felt so close to him." Her voice cracked, she was close to tears. She picked up her glass and drank half of it in one swallow. A few drops fell from the glass and landed on her dress.

"Hey you, careful you don't spill any more."

"It's not the wine I'm worried about spilling," she answered.

"Listen, you don't have to talk about anything if you don't want to." She sighed, a deep sigh.

"But I do," she whispered, desperately choking back tears now, refusing to give in to them. I gave her some time as she composed herself.

"What happened?" She closed her eyes and took a deep breath.

"We were at home, in one of our bedrooms playing dress up one afternoon, Lucy and I, like most kids do. Dad worked in sales for a textile company and he was away for a couple of days at some conference or another, so it was just us and Mum there to look after us. At some point I got bored, probably cos it was all too girly for me with all the pretty princess dress up stuff so I left Lucy to it. I was missing Dad, I hated it whenever he went away. He and I used to go fishing together. He'd bought me a fishing rod, a child's one which I loved cos I got to keep it next to his in the shed with all his other fishing gear. We had a tiny pond covered with a metal grill at the bottom of the garden, I used to take a little footstool and dangle the line of the rod into it, there weren't any fish in there but I didn't care. I just liked the feeling of calm it brought me as if it were the real thing. Of course it was a reminder of Dad and always made me look forward to the next time we'd go down to the river together.

"So I left Lucy, went downstairs and headed to the back door through the kitchen. My Mum was sitting at the dining room table reading or writing something, I can't remember which, she didn't ask what I was doing when I reached and took the shed key off the hook, she didn't even look up. I let myself out the back door, walked down the garden to Dad's shed and unlocked it."

I took a sip of wine and watched Gina intently.

"Anyway, Dad loved his carpentry, it was a bit of a hobby of his, so he's got all these tools everywhere, saws, planes, chisels, stuff like that, all scattered around on the top of his workbench in the middle of the room. I wanted to get to my fishing rod." Gina paused and looked away into the middle distance, for a while I thought she was going to bail on telling me the rest of the story after all, but after a few moments she continued. I noticed her hand was shaking. I held it. "Our rods were sat together on top of all these nets and bait boxes, I went over and picked mine up but as I went to pull it away it snagged on some netting. I yanked it. I went flying. I landed on my back halfway under the workbench. I laid there on my back for a minute just dazed. That's when I noticed it. An envelope, taped to the underside of the workbench."

Gina stopped again, her head bowed, eyes fixed on the sand

in front of her. Again, I waited for her to continue in her own time. When she did she spoke so quietly I could hardly hear her. "I reached up and pulled it down, then I got up off the floor. There were three photographs in there. They were of my Dad. He was with someone else, they were both naked…"

"The other person, it wasn't your Mum?"

"It wasn't my Mum, it wasn't anyone's mum. Not a woman, Mac. It was another man."

The words almost choked her as she looked up at me. "They were in different positions, I didn't understand, I was only eight years old Mac, for God's sake, I was only eight." Gina's voice cracked on the last word as she finally broke down. She began to sob.

"Christ, oh, G…" I did the only thing I could, which was to put my arm around her and pull her close to me doing my best to comfort her. We stayed together, embraced like this for a while, until her body stopped shaking and the tears finally subsided into silence.

"I'm sorry."

"Don't be, there's nothing to be sorry for," I answered, giving her shoulder a squeeze.

"Thank you Mac. For listening, I mean."

We sat in silence a while longer.

"Did you ever tell anyone, or confront your Dad over it?"

"No. You're the only person I've ever told."

"What did you do with the photos?"

"Tore them up into tiny pieces and buried them in the bottom of the bin. I didn't want to tell Mum or Lucy, I didn't know how to even begin to approach Dad about it, I wanted to protect him because I loved him but also a new part of me loathed him for this. When he came home, he obviously knew one of us must have found it. He never showed it though, must have killed him. I was the only one who changed towards him so he may have realised it was me. I didn't know how to deal with it, I was just a child. It took me until I was an adult to fully process it all. It really messed me up Mac, fucking hell, it really messed me up, for so many years."

"So you've never felt able to talk to him about it? Even now, as an adult?"

"He was diagnosed with pancreatic cancer when I was fifteen, he passed away a little over two months later. I didn't get chance."

"Oh God, I'm so sorry Gina."

"The sad thing is, he didn't do anything wrong, he didn't commit any crime, he was gay that was all and there's absolutely nothing wrong with that. Okay, so he had a family but he still loved us all, me, Lucy and Mum just the same, it didn't change that. He just had this other life. If he'd come out and told us, and I think at some point he would have, then it would have been a shock, maybe not to me, but in time we would have accepted it and understood it. As a family we would have gotten through and lived with it. Maybe we'd even have stayed together as a family."

"You should never have had to go through all that Gina, not as a kid, and definitely not all on your own." Gina turned to look at me.

"Thanks again Mac, not just for listening but for being here, and for going through all this nightmare stuff with me."

"Hey, anytime, what are friends for?" Gina stood up, swayed slightly and, with her bare feet caressed the sand in front of her with her toes as she looked out to sea.

"You know what I fancy? Another drink."

"Well there's no more wine sorry, best I can do is a black coffee back at mine."

"Sure," she said absently. I picked up my jacket, put it on and turned round to gather up the empty glasses. When I turned back, Gina was facing me wearing only tiny red panties and a matching lace bra. The dress she had unzipped lay pooled at her feet.

"I had a better idea," she said huskily. I looked at the dress, then up at Gina, then back at the dress.

"I'm guessing you're wanting to get that soak in?"

"Shut up and come here," she breathed as she stepped out of her dress.

I got to my feet and stood in front of her, she put her arms slowly around my neck and we shared our first kiss together with passion. It felt natural, almost like we had done this a million times before. As we laid back down in the softness of the warm sand, I wondered just what else friends were for.

CHAPTER SIXTEEN

I was awoken abruptly by the squealing laughter of children from somewhere outside my chalet the next morning. I reached for my phone and blinked until my bleary eyes were able to focus on the time displayed on the screen. I wasn't surprised to see it was almost eleven. Groggily I swung my legs out of bed and ran my hands through my hair a couple of times. The events of the night just gone quickly came flooding back. An image of her face, head back and eyes closed, breathing fast as she lay beneath. I seem to remember it being past half three when we finally got back to the camp. Our goodnight parting consisted of a bashful and slightly awkward peck on the cheek from Gina before I made my way back here and crashed.

I got up and threw on the same t-shirt and shorts that I'd been wearing, for most of the evening anyway, the night before. I badly needed a dose of caffeine in my system. I walked over to my tiny kitchen area, rinsed out my solitary mug and spooned one and a half teaspoons of strong coffee. I turned and surveyed my dishevelled appearance in the mirror while I waited for the kettle to boil. It dawned on me what I had done. What if last night has ruined our friendship? The rather awkward quick-peck kiss goodnight she'd given me had surely served as a hint that all might not be rosy for a while. That's not to make light of the fact that last night had been a highly emotionally charged one, for Gina anyway. I had been there to offer her solace and comfort as her friend.

Okay, after that you might say I'd gone above and beyond the call of duty but she had been the instigator of that, not me. I very much doubt my standing up and dropping my shorts to the sand in front of her would have had quite the same effect vice versa. What seemed almost certain was that Gina and I would agree that this would be, although not without feeling and sentiment, nonetheless a one night stand and as such should go no further than the two of us.

There was really no one to tell in any case, it's not as if, being both single, either one of us faced angry repercussions from a partner potentially finding out. Nonetheless, I couldn't push away the feeling of guilt.

I showered and changed, I felt fresher, revived and ready to make a decision. Clearly the best thing would be to do the gallant thing and go to Gina's right away and apologise for taking things too far. As if in disagreement my stomach rumbled loudly in protest. On the other hand, perhaps a full English first might be best. No reason to do this on an empty stomach after all. In fact, it was as good as lunch, might as well leave her until sometime this afternoon.

I picked up my wallet and went to leave, at the door I paused. I checked my reflection in the mirror once more, opened the door, looked left and right and left to make my way hastily out of the camp to find some breakfast somewhere on the edge of town. I made my way to a greasy spoon café and ordered a full English. A sizeable plateful of fatty, artery-clogging fried food left me feeling over full and slightly queasy.

A rumble of thunder mirrored my mood as I headed back

towards the camp, I hoped it wasn't some sort of omen. As I drew ever nearer, the guilt overcame me. It was time to bite the bullet, go and see her, there was no sense in putting it off any longer. She would surely be feeling the same way so why drag it out any longer than necessary.

"Mac, hey Mac, over here." I looked up to see Wayne at the entrance to the function room. He gestured for me to follow him and disappeared inside. Grateful for another distraction I followed him. I went through the door to see Leon. They both looked unhappy.

"Hey boys, how's my favourite couple? What's up?" I grinned.

"I suppose you already know, Gina quit."

My grin vanished and my breakfast churned in my stomach.

"Whoa, wait, what do you mean, quit?"

"She's quit the band, Mac. You mean you didn't know?"

"No I didn't, but hang on, wait, she was pretty upset about a few things last night, I'll go and see her, I'm sure she'll calm down and we can sort this out."

"Too late, she's gone. She packed up and left early this morning. She left a note at reception saying she had to leave right away due to some sort of family crisis and she wouldn't be able to complete the season. That's it. Done. She's not coming back."

Shit.

I hadn't seen this coming, I was gobsmacked.

I pulled up a chair and sat down heavily. Wayne and Leon followed suit.

"We kind of thought she might have told you last night

when you went off to talk to her? She didn't say anything?" Wayne asked.

"No, she didn't say anything at all about leaving, I can't believe she'd just walk out like this. What are we going to do? We're screwed."

"Nah," Leon replied, "Graham will call the agency, they'll send us someone else, sounds mercenary but there's always artists constantly looking for work, this is a pretty decent, well paid gig too, they'll be queuing up to get this one, trust me."

Alice had been right about that then, at least. We were simply agency paid music workers, our only requirement to be competent and show up every night. When people came to see Rebel Shout it wasn't just to see us and hear us play our songs, they came to be willing and active participants in the excitement of a rising new pop band. Here, at Clifton Sands Holiday Camp, people didn't come to see us, they came to dance to the songs we played. We were nobodies. Only it never felt that cold and clinical to us.

The four of us had formed a genuine friendship and camaraderie, we enjoyed being in each other's company. We laughed together. For that reason, the routine never became overly, well, routine. The difference between us and Rebel Shout may have been like night and day but in terms of personnel the bond was pretty much the same.

I was gutted Gina was gone. I had no doubt that she had left to go back and have some form of wedding impending confrontation with her family members. If this is what she felt she needed to do then she had to do what she had to do, I guess.

I couldn't help but feel disappointed that she had chosen not to speak with me about it, or even let me know she was leaving. Then again perhaps she felt she'd said enough last night, it's not like she owed me an explanation after all.

I decided, for the time being anyway, not to try to contact Gina. She knew where I was and had my number if she needed me. I needed time anyhow to let this sink in and get my head around it, and most likely so did she.

I roused myself from my thoughts and looked up at my two remaining band mates sat silently around the table. It was plain to see from their demeanour that they too were not unaffected by Gina's sudden departure.

"She might have bloody well said goodbye at least," announced Wayne, as if reading my mind. Neither Leon or I could think of any sort of insightful response to this so we lapsed back into morose silence once more.

"Shit, what about Graham anyway? He must be going absolutely mental over this isn't he?"

"You'd think so but actually, no, quite the opposite in fact, he and Gina didn't exactly see eye to eye did they? Sounds harsh but I think he's pretty pleased to see the back of her quite honestly." I nodded slowly. I guess not, after all. Graham most likely considered the inconvenience well worth it.

"He was straight on the case as soon as he heard the news, says he'll get us together when he hears back about a new singer from the agency."

Wayne was right. True to his word, later that afternoon Graham called us to a band meeting with news of Gina's impending replacement. I realised that I would have to join Leon and Wayne in adopting a professional, 'show must go on' attitude if I was to get over Gina being gone. Graham was already waiting for us as we each took seats around the table.

"Okay boys listen up, as you all know, following the untimely and frankly bloody selfish departure of the last singer I've been on to the agency for an immediate replacement. Now for your precious sakes I've enquired after the closest match to Gina they've got and they're sending us this one, local girl, here you go, she knows the set list and she should be here any time soon to try out."

The three of us looked collectively down at the portfolio, it encompassed a not inconsiderable resumé that included stints singing in wedding bands, nightclubs and several residencies aboard a cruise liner. It also included was a glossy eight by ten photo of a smiling, rosy-cheeked girl with bouffant blonde hair wearing a garish cream sequinned blouse and holding a microphone to her mouth. She had a sizeable gap between her two front teeth.

"Who is she then?" said Wayne.

"Erm... Debbie," I read, "Debbie Valentine. Says she's twenty-five."

Right on cue the doors at the far end of the room swung open, we all looked up in unison as the lady in question stepped through. She was wearing a fashionably smart, semi-formal blazer jacket over a tight white blouse that appeared to contain her generously endowed bosom with quite some considerable strain. Ditto the material of the tight knee length skirt that struggled, under duress against the flesh of her equally generously endowed rear end. The blonde bouffant hairstyle remained, but she was clearly ten to fifteen years older than her portfolio photograph.

"Shirley fucking Valentine more like," Leon said under his breath. "'If she's twenty-five, I'm Danny La Rue."

"Beggars can't be choosers, Leon," hissed Graham. The three of us sat in awkward silence as Graham regaled Debbie with his welcome pitch.

"Be nice," whispered Wayne.

"Always, darling."

Debbie, as it turned out was every bit as bold and brassy as her appearance suggested. She was not in the least bit intimidated by the likes of us. She called each of us 'babes' during the course of introductions and frequently let out a loud, high pitched, machine gun laugh at the end of most sentences. She had a larger than life persona that was infectious. I quite liked her. I was sure she would win over Wayne and Leon too, although right now it was difficult to gauge exactly quite what they were thinking. Gina would have hated her, of that I was certain. Graham smoothly moved proceedings along from introductions to Debbie's audition.

I noted that rather than do his usual disappearing act at this point, Graham hovered near the entrance, clearly keen to see and hear for himself. As we took the stage, Leon turned on the PA and gave our would be new singer a quick mic check. I sighed at the strangeness of seeing a different female standing in Gina's spot.

"Are you ready Debbie?" asked Wayne.

"Whenever you are babes," she chirped back cheerfully. Wayne counted us in and we began the first of three songs. By the end of song one it was clear that she would get the job. It wasn't that she had a great voice, it wasn't a match on what Gina could do, she just had the showmanship. Replacing Gina with Debbie was a bit like taking a sleek, sports car and swapping it for a reasonably priced hatchback. One may have been far more pleasurable to drive and of higher value compared to the other, a trusty old family faithful, but in essence both would get the job done. Debbie was an experienced and capable singer. That was all that Clifton Sands needed.

"Bravo! Bravo! Congratulations my dear, you've got the job!" enthused Graham. He clearly overlooked any need to consult the three of us, as he strode back to the stage towards her.

Debbie gave a little look to the heavens before raising a balled fist upwards and bringing it down in a chain yanking gesture of triumph.

"Yes! Smashed it!" She said in celebration.

Leon, Wayne and I stepped forward to offer our own, more modest congratulations. She gratefully hugged each of us in turn with a squeal of delight.

"Marvellous stuff! Now come on love, let's get you over to the office and signed up."

"See you tomorrow night boys! Can't wait! We'll kick some arse!" With one last shrill squeal of laughter she disappeared out of the door with Graham. The three of us stood in silence for a moment gazing at the exit door.

"Well, what did we make of that?" said Wayne.

"It was a bit like being in a *Carry On* film wasn't it? I kept expecting her blouse to burst open and her bra to fly off and smack me in the face," answered Leon.

The following night Debbie took the stage for her debut as our new singer. With the confidence of a seasoned performer, she chatted with audience members between songs and occasionally indulged in slightly risqué banter with some. Nonetheless she gave us an altogether more 'seaside' feel as a band.

Although Debbie would only be with us for the remaining five weeks, Wayne and Leon still felt a customary obligation to offer a celebratory after show drinks to welcome Debbie to the group. Just as before, we sat around the same table and drank the same bottle of Prosecco. Debbie was somehow louder once she had a couple of drinks inside her.

"So Debbie, is singing what you do all year round?" asked Wayne.

"Oh yes babes, mostly, but not all the time, not anymore, too much of a strain on the old pipes at my age."

"Just a part time thing then?" I said.

"That's right my love, my husband works, of course, he's a civil servant, but I do other stuff to chip in, I like to keep busy with some other jobs, you know, voice coach, cocktail maker, sex worker…" She giggled.

The last job title made us all stop as though we were playing musical statues. No one dared to move.

"Erm, sex worker?" Leon was brave.

"Yes, just at weekends that one, if I'm not out singing of

course." Another ominous silence followed as we waited to hear Debbie crack up laughing at such an obvious joke and tell us we should have seen the looks on our faces. She did neither. After a few seconds, however, she did seem to clock that we appeared somewhat taken aback by her admission. "Oh I don't mean I sell my body or nothin' like that. I ain't a prossie, don't worry!" she laughed.

"What do you do then?" I asked, someone had to.

"The sex chat babes, the ones on the phone lines. The customer rings the premium number in his mag, it gets connected through to me at home and I just sit there on the other end telling him everything he wants to hear for as long as I can keep him on the line. The longer I can keep him talking the more money I make. That's it, piece of cake really."

"Blimey, I didn't know phone sex was still, you know, a thing."

"What do they want to talk about?" asked Leon, somewhat naively.

"Well obviously I don't never give out any personal details and they don't see my number so it's all safe. If they do start getting a bit weird and funny I'll just hang up, but most of 'em are just lonely pervs wanting to know if I'm wearing frilly knickers, suspenders and stockings or what have you. Some of 'em want me to tell 'em what I'm doing to myself, stuff like that. Course, I never tell 'em what I'm actually doing though."

"And what would you actually be doing?"

"Well, last time I was sat on the sofa in my dressing gown and slippers watching *Antiques Roadshow* with the sound off."

I stifled a laugh.

"What about your husband though, I mean, does he know about this?" asked Leon, Debbie looked bemused.

"Of course he does babes, it's his favourite programme, we watch it together."

"I meant the sex chat thing, not bloody *Antiques Roadshow*."

"Oh that? It was his idea actually! He loves me talkin' dirty does Martin, got a gift for it he says, he said I'd be a natural and guess what? Hey ho, what can I say!" She cackled.

"I see, well, no sense wasting good talent I guess."

"So, anyhow I'm guessing you two golden oldies have been doing this forever but what's a handsome young buck like you doing playing in a group of fuddies like this?"

"Me? Oh well, you know, it's really just a summer job for me, like a one off, you know." I avoided eye contact with the boys.

"Oh really? So what was it you were doing before then my lovely?"

"'Well, I… I used to be a musician."

"And now you're in a function band!"

Debbie laughed.

Ouch.

Her phone buzzed. "That'll be Martin," she reached down, revealing rather a colossal amount of cleavage. She held up the retrieved phone and squinted at the text, the light from the screen illuminating her face as she read the message. "Right, looks like my chariot's here, I'm gonna have to love you and leave you I'm afraid."

"Okay, well once again, welcome aboard Debbie, great first show."

"Ah, thank you babes, I was born to do this, you know. I'm in my element up there alright, don't you worry about that boys." With that she blew each of us a theatrical kiss and made her way off into the night.

"There she goes, the singing sex worker," Leon said once she was out of sight.

"She didn't put that in the CV did she."

CHAPTER SEVENTEEN

Over the next few weeks I began to realise just how much more of a routine being in this band really was without Gina. With no disrespect to Leon and Wayne, or even to Debbie, I missed the level of class that Gina had brought. One good thing about Debbie was that she was never anything less that happy. Debbie didn't have mood swings, in fact she only seemed to have the one, and that was to be almost relentlessly happy and cheerful. Inevitably though, the days in the camp and performances at night came to feel mundane. Without Gina around, I no longer had that someone to talk to. I no longer had a singer to admire and enjoy an onstage rapport with. Consequently, the days tended to drag, sometimes to the point where I would find myself willing the evening and show time to hurry up and get here, only to return to the chalet afterwards without a single significant or meaningful memory of the performance. I was now almost fully on auto pilot, just a functioning member of a function band.

I thought about Gina constantly. I wondered where she was and what she was up to. Sometimes not knowing caused me to worry about her and to blame myself for the part I played in her leaving in the manner of which she did. Most of all I just missed her. The level of hurt that I felt by her leaving made me start to question just what my feelings were towards her. I never usually felt this low about a friendship coming to an end, maybe I did feel more for her. I was confused. I grew slightly resentful in some ways that she clearly didn't feel the need to contact me. It might have been slightly pathetic, childish even, but I felt abandoned by her. There was nothing to stop me texting or calling her. Nothing except pride anyway. No, if she wanted to talk to me, she would have got in touch. It wasn't for me to go chasing after her like some sad, lovesick puppy. Instead it was time to start thinking about moving on. Time to start thinking about me. When our last performance of the season arrived, it took place and ended without any great fanfare. Debbie announced to the by now dwindling audience that this was our final night and that it had all been wonderful, but only a smattering of applause in return showed that it meant little to most of them.

I said my last goodbye to Debbie and told her it had been fun. I hoped to see her again some time. She gave me a rib crushing bear hug in response along with a messy wet kiss on the cheek that left me with what felt like half my face covered in red lipstick. The boys I had already arranged to meet for one last goodbye drink tomorrow lunchtime.

Once back at my chalet I undressed and stared up to the ceiling in darkness. The last twelve weeks or so at Clifton Sands had been anything but what I had expected it to be. My time as a seaside holiday camp performer was at an end. I had anticipated the entire period to consist of a day to day routine of keeping my head down. I had intended to keep as lower profile as possible, in short, everyday crawl from under stone, play gig, take money, crawl back under stone. Repeat every day for twelve weeks till done, go home and let us never fucking speak of this time again. Ever.

How I was wrong. So wrong. The journey instead had been more like the rollercoaster down on the seafront. I had met two gay men in their late thirties with bald spots and paunches that would become my mates for life. I'd formed another friendship with someone else that would end shortly after in sad and desperate tragedy. I'd become acquainted with a man who I'd come to regard as my nemesis who would turn out to be my saviour in my time of need. I'd almost had my heart stolen back by the woman who'd done her best to break it only months earlier. I'd won money, lost face, been both lauded and berated, fought, laughed, cried and, for one night only, even found time to find one night of passion with Gina. Ah, yes, Gina. The person that was my friend, my bandmate and my lover and yet remained estranged from all three. Maybe our paths would cross again someday, maybe further down the line, or maybe not ever. Perhaps what we shared in our brief time together would always be just a memory to the both of us. But, time waits for no man. I had money in the bank, a big city to return to and a future to plan. My train left tomorrow. I closed my eyes and drifted slowly off into a comfortable sleep. A loud bleep on my phone disturbed me.

It read:

'Meet me at the cafe tomorrow morning? Ten o'clock?'

I stared at the screen, blinking my eyes as another quickly followed.

'Please.'

It was from Gina.

CHAPTER EIGHTEEN

I awoke the following morning to the sound of heavily pouring rain outside. The summer was truly coming to an end in a clattering crescendo. I picked up my phone and looked at the time. Seven twenty. Virtually still the middle of the night for me. Still, little chance of dozing off again now.

I replied:

'Okay.'

Not a dream then. Curiosity may have killed the cat but I was willing to take my chances, such was my desire to hear what she had to say. With plenty of time to spare I rose and took a long shower. Thoughts on our impending meeting went through my head as I wiped clear the steam from the tiny square mirror above the sink in order to shave. The way I saw it, in all likelihood this meeting would play out in one of two possible scenarios. Gina would apologise for her actions before wishing me farewell over the course of a cup of coffee. Or, Gina would refuse to apologise for her actions before wishing me farewell over the course of a cup of coffee. I still wanted to know why she'd left either way.

The rain had calmed down by the time I pulled on my jacket to leave. As I walked, I couldn't help feeling a certain sense of trepidation.

I arrived, it occurred to me that I had not been back here since Gina had left. Butterflies flitted momentarily through my stomach. Instinctively I already knew where she would be sitting. I looked over and there she was, sat wearing a black beret and red leather jacket with her hands wrapped either side around a cup of, I assumed, chai latte. She gave me a small wave and a slightly nervous smile. Perhaps it wasn't just me feeling a little that way then. I ordered an Americano and stood for a few minutes, awkwardly waiting for it to be made. Once done I picked up my coffee and walked over to the table.

"Hello Mac."

"Hello Gina."

"How are you?"

"Good, I'm good thanks. You?"

"Yes I'm fine thanks." A slightly awkward silence followed. Gina took a breath.

"Thank you for coming to meet me." I nodded.

"You're a little late if you've come for your job back." Gina smiled ruefully.

"No, well obviously not. Besides, you sound pretty good as you are with the new girl singing."

"Oh? And where did you hear that?"

"I heard for myself, last night when I came to watch you." My eyes widened in surprise.

"You were here last night, at the camp?"

"Well it wasn't by satellite link was it? So yes, obviously."

"Oh right, sorry, foolishly I just thought that you might have taken the time then to come and say hello to us, but I was forgetting that's probably a difficult word for you to say isn't it? A bit like goodbye."

Gina picked up her coffee, sat back in her chair and stirred it absently with her spoon. She must have anticipated that it wouldn't be too long before the conversation turned to this.

"I wasn't there very long, only for about three songs, then I had to go. And yes I did stay out of sight I admit. I've been back in Edmouth for a few days now so I've been in and out of the camp a number of times while I've been here if you want to know."

"Really? Why's that?"

"Sorting some stuff, that's all."

"Well, don't give me a straight answer whatever you do, will you?"

"Sorting my life out, Mac, okay? That's why I'm here."

"So come on then, why did you just walk out Gina? Without a word to me, or anyone else for that matter?" Gina took a deep breath this time before answering.

"I left the way I did because my head was a complete mess that's why, I had to get away. There's been so much going on, far more than you know Mac and it all got a whole lot more complicated after I went, I can promise you that."

"Okay, I can understand that but what about all the personal stuff you told me, I thought we shared something that night? Like, actual meaningful stuff? Not to mention after all that, when we…"

"That doesn't mean I owed you an explanation. I don't owe you anything," she interrupted. I felt the colour rise in my face at this rebuke and a red mist quickly descended.

"No, no, of course not, that's fine, you're right, why should I think I might have deserved a goodbye? Clearly I'm no one special but hey, at least you made sure we went out with a bang, eh?"

"Don't be a prick Mac, please. I don't want the memory of our night together cheapened." She said quietly. I looked away out the window. "Look, believe it or not it really hurt to leave without saying a word to you, or Leon and Wayne for that matter. I'm not always the heartless cow you think I am you know, you all mean a lot to me but if I'd sent you a goodbye text then of course you'd have replied, no doubt wanting answers to questions. I'd have tried to find some sort of way to reply and it would have all turned into one big, awkward, messy conversation. A conversation I didn't want to have. Not even with you, Mac, sorry."

"I see, okay, well I guess that's fair enough," I replied, the frostiness in me thawing out a little. We both remained quiet for a moment.

"I have missed you, you know."

"Yes, well that's understandable." Gina smiled. "I've missed you too."

"How are the boys?" asked Gina.

"Ah you know, same old Wayne and Leon, still the original bickering couple. They've missed you too. Graham, not so much."

"Oh god, well I've missed him too, like a dose of the clap."

"That's a delightful comparison."

"Yeah, well, I'm sure the feeling is mutual don't worry."

"G, listen, please don't think I'm prying or anything ok, because I'm not. Whatever you left to get sorted, well, did you, you know, get it sorted?" Gina sighed.

"In part yes. I've been staying with an old friend, Lydia, in London for the last few weeks. She was my best friend at college and she's been wonderful. She gave me some good, level headed advice that settled me down until I was ready to go and do what I left Edmouth to do, which was to go and see Richard and Lucy."

"And did you?"

"Yes. Yes I did, I think I managed to close that chapter. It wasn't until a few weeks later, after that, that the mother of all bombshells got dropped."

"What happened?"

"A trip to see the doctor, that's what happened."

"Oh God, no, tell me it isn't anything serious."

"Oh, I'm afraid it's serious alright. Very serious, but I'm not ill." I frowned and shook my head slightly as we continued to look at each other.

"I'm pregnant, Mac."

You know that scene in the movie *Jaws* where Chief Brody is sat in his chair facing the sea on a crowded beach when he suddenly witnesses the shark attack happen in the water right in front of him? You know how the background rushes forward as the camera pans in on his horror stricken face? You could have used exactly the same effect on me as I sat, frozen.

"Pregnant? Are you... are you sure?"

"Yes, I'm sure."

"I mean definitely though, is it definite? Are you definitely sure?" I spluttered.

"Definitely sure." I sat back in my chair and ran my fingers through my hair with both hands. "I don't love you Gina."

"I don't love you either Mac."

"Well, what the hell are we going to do?"

"Well, I'm going to go off and have a baby, that's what I'm going to do. It's okay, you don't have to do anything. You're not the father."

A mixture of relief and mass confusion flooded through me. My mind halted, backtracked and began to race around in circles like a headless chicken as it desperately tried to process the information.

"I'm not? I'm not the father?" Gina shook her head. A further silence passed between us and then, in a moment of spectacular clarity, it finally came to me. "Oh no, it's Richard isn't it? You went back and slept with Richard to get back at your sister and now you're pregnant with his child. That's it, isn't it? Oh Gina, Jesus Christ, what were you thinking?"

"No I bloody didn't sleep with Richard! I'm not a complete slut thank you very much! What a typical, bloody shallow, male minded response." Instantly silenced by this, I swiftly dismounted off of my high horse. Confusion returned.

"But… but I don't understand Gina? You just said it's not me, and now you're saying you didn't sleep with Richard, so who else?"

"Carlos is the father, Mac. I'm having Carlos' baby." If I thought I'd been shocked before, I couldn't be more so now if you'd stuck a wired cable up my arse and plugged me directly into the National Grid.

"Carlos?" Gina nodded.

"We've actually been seeing each other, pretty much the whole time more or less since I started at the camp."

"You and Carlos?"

"Yes.

"Carlos? The Carlos?"

"Yes! Will you stop saying his fucking name for Christ's sake."

"I'm dreaming aren't I? This is all a dream and I'm going to wake up soon in my own bed and laugh out loud at just how ridiculous…"

"Mac, stop, please. And yes I'm bloody sure before you start."

I looked at Gina as the news sunk in. Her eyes were pleading now, the earlier tone of confidence had been replaced now by a look of uncertainty and vulnerability.

"Does he know?" I asked quietly. Gina nodded.

"He knows. We've spent all this week discussing it. We're going to go and live in Spain; his parents have left him a business property out there. We're going to move out and take it over."

"You and the most unpopular man in Edmouth? I just can't believe it, you and him together, a couple all this time, in secret? I just can't get my head round it, G. I'm having a hard time understanding how on earth you two even got together."

"It was my choice to keep it secret because I knew people wouldn't understand. You don't know him like I know him Mac, I know what everybody else thinks of him, that he's just an obnoxious brute, and yes okay, I know he can be. He understands me and believe it or not he does care about me, and he can be kind."

"Well I guess you'd be sure of that now, after you've known him, what, a whole three months?"

"Yes, exactly the same amount of time I'd have known you if you were the father."

"And how do you know I'm not the father Gina? How do you know the baby is his and not mine exactly?"

"I just know Mac, alright? I feel it, a woman knows these things."

"A woman knows these things? Really? And that constitutes medical proof does it?"

"It's all I need to know, yes."

"Yeah? Well what about a paternity test, has Carlos taken one?"

"No he hasn't, tell you what, I'll go and ask him shall I? Excuse me Carlos, do you mind taking a paternity test before we go? Only I slept with Mac a few weeks ago, best to be sure eh? I'm not sure he'd be very fucking chuffed about that, do you?"

"I take it he doesn't know about me?"

"I don't think I'd be sitting here talking to you right now if he did, do you? More likely you'd be lying in a hospital bed sucking your breakfast through a straw."

I can't believe she cheated on him, after everything we had talked about. I had cheated him too I guess, I was mad she had made me a part of this.

"I'm just not sure if you really know what you're doing here, Gina? How do you know you're not just making a mistake?" Gina laughed bitterly.

"My whole life's been a mess of crazy mistakes Mac! Don't you see? Finally I have a chance to move away and leave the past behind, once and for all. This is the biggest decision of my life, alright? I'm gonna take this chance and I'm gonna give every last bit of my heart and soul to make sure it works. The two of us are going to go away, have our baby, start a whole new life and live happily fucking ever after, okay?"

"Just like one big, happy family, eh?"

I saw how much the impact of these few words stung Gina. Tears welled up in her eyes and I instantly regretted saying them.

"Yes. That's right, because everyone deserves to be happy in life, Mac. Even someone who's fucked up as many times as I have in mine." Gina took a napkin off the table and began dabbing at her eyes. I held her hand.

"You're right. I'm sorry. You will make it work, I'm sure of it."

"Look, it's okay, I didn't ask you here because I wanted your validation Mac, or even your blessing. I just wanted you to know that's all, and hopefully for you to understand."

I nodded and looked down at my coffee cup, the dregs of which had grown cold. I looked back up at Gina.

"You want a refill?" Gina shook her head.

"No, thanks."

"When do you leave?"

"In a couple of hours. I've been staying in a little B&B in town, I'm packed and ready. Carlos is picking me up in a taxi and we're going straight to the airport."

"That's quick."

"Will you walk me back to my hotel?" I smiled and nodded.

"Love to."

The rain had stopped and the sun was trying it's best to come out as we left the café.

"So what actually happened then, when you met up with Richard and Lucy?"

"I went to their apartment, I'd made up my mind to confront the issue, really. I still had to psyche myself up, I mean I felt horribly nervous. I had gone over everything I wanted to say so many times. It was like I was rehearsing some bad movie scene. Once I rang the doorbell and Richard opened the door a complete calm came over me. It helped that he looked a hell of a lot more petrified than I did when he saw it was me. He looked like he'd seen a ghost. Lucy appeared behind him almost straight away and said something like 'what the bloody hell are you doing here?' Then she remembered herself a little bit and grudgingly asked me in. I declined. Then I basically told them that I hadn't come to cause trouble, I'd actually come to wish them well and tell them their future had my blessing. I said that whilst I could never forgive them for what they've done, I wasn't going to live the rest of my life hating them either. I told them I wouldn't be attending the wedding, no way in hell I was going to that, then I said I was going away and they'd not likely be seeing me again for quite some time."

"Blimey, how did they take that?"

"Well they didn't tell me to stick my blessing up my arse which I half expected them to. Lucy seemed more freaked out cos she thought I meant I was going to go and chuck myself off a bridge or something, so I had to reassure the pair of them that I really was just moving away."

"Right, and that was it?"

"Well, pretty much. There wasn't a whole lot of small talk to be had as you can imagine."

"Do you think you might get back in touch with them at some point further down the line?"

"Maybe. Right now I just need the distance from them Mac, I'm going to go to Spain and start a family. I need them to go away and get married. Then sometime in the future perhaps, when all the shit storms this has caused have all blown over, died down and settled, we can possibly get back in to touch somehow and, I don't know, start to rebuild some bridges, heal some wounds, you know? We'll see I guess."

I nodded and we walked on. We arrived at Gina's Bed and Breakfast hotel. A short pathway to the front door lay in the middle of a tiny but immaculately manicured front garden. The net curtain swished aside on the corner of the downstairs window and the face of a little old lady with round spectacles peered out. I took her to be the landlady. Upon recognising Gina as one of her guests she smiled curtly and gave a quick wave before disappearing back out of view as the curtain closed. Gina waved back before turning to face me.

"I guess this is it then," she said.

"I guess so." We looked at each other for a moment before Gina stepped forward, put her arms around me and hugged me tightly. I hugged her back. The scent of her hair and neck reminded me of our night together on the beach, a night that seemed a very long time ago now.

"I will be in touch Mac, okay? Not for a few months, maybe not until, you know, I've got some news to share with you."

"Whenever you feel ready, whenever you want, but hey, listen, I'm here if you need anything."

"Thank you, I appreciate that."

"Good luck with everything, Gina."

"Thanks. Sorry, look, I'm shit at goodbyes. I'm gonna go now before this gets awkward. Goodbye, Mac, take care." With that she leaned forward and kissed me on the cheek. I watched her go.

"Do you have a spare room in this new place? If not tell Carlos he'll need to build me something for when I come to visit, nothing special, just a small annexe, something with an en suite would be nice?"

"I think you could be in for a long wait there."

"See ya."

"See ya."

Then she was gone.

CHAPTER NINETEEN

On the walk back to the camp I had a strange mix of emotions. My mind buzzed at the sheer amount of news it had been asked to take in. Gina being pregnant was one thing but finding out the man she proposed to be the father of her unborn child was none other than Carlos. At first it seemed almost incomprehensible, but now, as the initial shock of this revelation began to wear off, I began to realise that their coupling, and indeed their mutual attraction was perhaps not quite as surprising as I had first thought. Opposites attract I guess. To be honest, they have similarities. They are both ready for a good argument.

I can't speak for Leon or Wayne, but when I thought back now to the various scenarios involving Gina and Carlos it had not once occurred to me that they were involved together, but now it all kind of made sense. Perhaps it was strength of character that drew Gina to Carlos and vice versa. She said he had a kind and caring side and, although pretty much everyone else who knew him would have found that hard to believe, she must see it in him. There's plenty of men out there who would have run a mile upon hearing the pregnancy announcement. Gina could have found herself shunned and forced to face a very uncertain future alone. To his credit, Carlos had not run. Instead he stepped up to the plate, big time. Respect to him for that. I'd have shit myself.

Thankfully now this meant I had the confidence and reassurance that Gina would be looked after. God only knows what that must have meant to her. At least I could move on now from this situation, safe in the knowledge it isn't mine.

Well, almost, but not quite.

One giant, fat elephant still left in the proverbial room. Gina might be having my baby. She might think she knows but she can't be completely sure. She knew it, I knew it. Nope, this was Gina one hundred per cent burying her head firmly in the sand on this one. Who could blame her? Carlos had everything to offer her and the child. I wouldn't have been able to offer her anything. Sad but true. While I did want to know, I knew I could never put Gina through the tests. It could still turn out to be Carlos' child after all, then everything would have been destroyed for her for nothing. No, the best thing for everybody was for me to do exactly as Gina had done and bury my own head in the sand. I took a deep breath and sighed.

As I returned to Clifton Sands, still deep in thought, I barely noticed the taxi parked with its boot open, engine running, just inside the entrance. As I drew nearer, the boot was brought down and sharply closed. It was Carlos. As if my heart hadn't had enough for one day. He walked up and placed his hand on the passenger side door handle. Our eyes met as he looked up to see it was me, he paused and stared. Emotionless. Then, without a word, he opened the taxi door, heaved his giant frame into the passenger seat and slammed it shut. No big hug and tearful farewell from him then.

I met Leon and Wayne for one last goodbye drink in the function room bar that afternoon. I felt a strange pang of melancholy at this as I walked over to them. They were sat on the same table as they had been when I first met them. They both looked up and smiled warmly as I approached.

"Hi boys, so what are we having? What's our last good drink together gonna be? Tequila slammers all round? Cocktails?"

I thought how funny it would have been if Gina were sat here now to offer her a Sex on the Beach from the cocktail menu. I could just picture her death stare. Maybe not. I chuckled to myself anyway.

"Actually I'll just have a bitter lemon please Mac."

"Half a mild, thanks."

"Well, you sure are cheap dates." I had made up my mind before arriving here that I would keep the news about Gina and Carlos to myself. I returned to my seat and handed my two friends their drinks. Having mostly discussed our future plans with each other leading up to this point we all fell into what amounted to little more than small talk in an oddly anticlimactic way. Wayne and Leon apparently always took themselves off on holiday as a reward at the end of the season. Everyone it seemed was heading abroad, except me.

"Have you decided where you're jetting off to this year yet then?" Leon looked across at Wayne before replying.

"Well, we were thinking maybe one of the Greek islands weren't we?"

"Domestos?" I asked with a grin.

"Domestos? You silly twat," laughed Wayne.

"Never mind, he can think of us sipping gin and tonics on sun beds in matching Speedos in the sun whilst he's shivering in smoggy old London town, can't he," grinned Leon.

"Speaking of which, what time is your train back to the big smoke?"

"Ten past four."

"Yeah, well, we'll have to be off in a bit ourselves too."

We chatted for a while longer and finished our drinks when sure enough, the boys stood up, announcing it was time they were going.

"So, see you again in nine months, I hope?"

"Well you never know, nine months is a long time." Long enough to have a baby I couldn't help thinking.

"Well the door stays open to you on this one. The job is yours until you say otherwise, Graham has already agreed."

"Thanks boys, that means a lot, it really does, I appreciate it."

"Take care won't you, Mac?"

"I will, you too, keep in touch, okay!"

"Will do."

We each exchanged hugs, I watched as they got into their battered VW Beetle and drove out of the car park. With a final wave they too were gone.

Just me left then.

With nothing else left to do but pack up the last of my things, I slowly turned away and made my way back towards my cabin to do just that. On my way I passed by the prettier of the flower bed areas that adorned the pathway on my route. I paused by the red maple tree. A plaque at the base read:

In Loving Memory of Matthew Daley

I squatted down and brushed a small amount of earth away

from the lettering. Adios Amigo, rest easy, my friend.

When I arrived back at my cabin, I packed and cleaned the place up. Arriving and departing with limited belongings. I still had the best part of an hour to kill till I had to be at the station. I decided I may as well go back and sit in the function room bar. I locked my door and said a farewell to my humble abode.

As I entered the function room, I found the bar closed and indeed the entire room deserted. Of course, it always closed at this time after lunch, I forgot. Oh well. I took down a wooden chair turned upright on a nearby table and placed it on the floor. I sat down in the silence of the cavernous room. The clouds broke outside and shafts of late summer sunlight streamed through the tall glass windows. It illuminated a million floating dust particles in the air. Facing the stage, I stared straight at it, falling into an almost trance like state as a daydream montage of memories from the place in front of me flickered inside and played out in my head. Damn, three months had passed so quick, it felt like a blur.

The doors behind me were pushed open, breaking both the silence and the spell. I snapped my head round to see it was only Elena.

"Oh, sorry Mr Mac, I didn't see you sitting there, I have to finish here and lock up doors now, sorry."

"Hi Elena, that's okay, I was about to leave anyway."

She smiled and wedged the door open before going back outside. When she returned she was pushing the soapy water contents of a black plastic bucket along the floor with a large mop. Reluctantly, I got up. Elena passed me slopping water onto the floor.

"Bollocks," she muttered under her breath.

"Good to hear your English is really coming on," I chuckled.

"One tries ones best," she mimicked a posh accent. "Is your last day today, eh? You look sad."

"Yes, I leave today, am I sad to go? Yeah, maybe a little, sure."

"Where you going? Back to your Mamma's house?"

"Yes," I replied a little self-conscious at that confession. "Back to my Mamma's house in the big smoke."

"London?"

"Yeah, that's right."

"I don't think I like London."

"Oh really? Why's that?" Elena leaned on her mop and appeared to give this question some consideration.

"I think because is big shit hole."

"Right. I see."

"Too noisy, too dirty. I like here, air is clean, sea is nice. Reminds me of home, only colder."

With that she walked over to the bar, squeezed out the mop, emptied the bucket into the sink and placed them both in a tall cupboard behind the bar. Then she took off her long cleaner's coat and hung it on a hook in a small alcove just out of view. When she stepped out of the bar I could see she was dressed in her plain clothes. As she came closer towards me she paused as she reached behind her neck and took out her hair band. She bent forward and shook her hair out before tossing it back over her neck and shoulders, it settled to give her a sudden wild look. I had never seen Elena beyond her cleaner guise before now. I was taken back. She caught my gaze and looked at me with a cross between bewilderment and concern.

"You okay, Mister Mac?"

"Yes… er… yes fine," I replied, recovering myself a little. "Ladies first." I gestured for her to walk ahead of me. As she did she slipped on the small soapy puddle she'd spilt moments ago, and with a sudden gasp fell backwards. In a flash I lunged forward, and with a deftness that surprised even me, caught her neatly in my arms. We stared at each other.

"Are you okay?"

"I think so." For a split second we remained in this position, like a figure skating couple at the end of their routine. Minus all the grace and poise of course. I raised her up till she was standing upright again in front of me, reluctantly I took my hands away from her slender arms. Our eyes remained locked together.

Breathe Mac, breathe.

"Elena, I don't suppose you'd like to… Would you like to join me for a cup of coffee?"

She smiled at me and held my gaze.

"No, sorry. I have boyfriend." The bubble filled with romantic hope burst instantly with a loud, metaphorical squelch.

"Boyfriend, sorry, I… I didn't know."

You bloody fool Mac. Why wouldn't a girl like this have a boyfriend? Elena was giggling. I looked up.

"Sorry, I make joke, no boyfriend. It's just that, just you never notice me before."

As I stood looking back at her, I realised I hadn't noticed her before. I had seen her kindness, her empathy, her jokes. She even went to Matt's funeral with me, but I hadn't seen her. How did I not notice her before? I had overlooked how many times her sense of humour made me laugh and how much I actually enjoyed being in her company. I hadn't noticed how truly beautiful she was before this moment.

Idiot.

"It's okay, I'm not really in the mood for coffee anyway, but thanks." She walked the rest of the way over to the exit. I could only look on after her.

"Sure, some other time maybe." I answered forlornly. She paused at the doorway to look back at me.

"Maybe not coffee, but cocktail? There is new cocktail bar in high street, it looks nice. You wanna go instead?"

I didn't need asking a second time. Cocktails in the middle of the afternoon? Hell yeah. To be honest if she'd suggested going off to drink goose fat together I'd have agreed just as eagerly. I threw on my jacket and by the time I joined her at the door my own smile had turned into a mile wide grin.

Never in my life have I been so happy to miss a train.

CHAPTER TWENTY

Nine months later

Interview article taken from *London Music Scene* magazine:

Hotly tipped new London band Enemy Mine have announced the recruitment of guitarist Dalian McIntyre to their ranks. The move sees the groups bassist/singer Jase Edwards reunited with his former band mate, the two having previously been members of Rebel Shout, another band from the capital who briefly enjoyed chart success.

Enemy Mine, who've have just signed a worldwide deal with Griffin Records following several successful showcase gigs in the city, are planning some UK and European dates next month, before moving on to Los Angeles to begin work on their debut album. We caught up with newly engaged Dalian for a quick chat at the band's rehearsal studio.

I: Hi Dalian, first of all congratulations on the new band and the recent engagement! You must feel blessed right now?
D: Thank you, yes I do indeed!
I: It must be a very exciting time for you right now, how did you hook up with the new band?
D: Well actually I'm indebted to an old acquaintance of mine for tipping me off that Jase was looking for a guitarist and was trying to track me down. We'd parted on good terms after

Rebel split so when I heard, I jumped at the chance. Lucky I kept his number!

I: What are the band's immediate plans?

D: Well, right now we're busy rehearsing for this upcoming tour, it's a chance for our audience to get to know us and hear some of the new songs live before we go to LA to record the album.

I: Will you be playing She's on It?

D: No! (*laughs*)

I: Rebel Shout were dropped after one single, that must have been tough for you and Jase to take, how did you bounce back from that?

D: It wasn't an easy time for sure, there weren't too many immediate options for me.

I: Is it true you actually took a job playing in a holiday camp band somewhere shortly after?

D: Absolutely true, and you know what? I learned more from my time in that band than I did playing in Rebel Shout. It taught me you can find happiness in both success and failure sometimes in life. It's where I met my fiancé, an actual Greek goddess, and where I made a few life friends along the way. I still have a great affection for the place, who knows maybe we'll do a secret gig there one day! (*laughs again*)

Enemy Mine are expected to release their debut album later in the year and begin their UK tour in July with a warmup gig in, as yet undisclosed venue, rumoured to be in the seaside town of Edmouth.

ACKNOWLEDGEMENTS

I would very much like to thank the following people for their support in the writing and publication of this book.

Mum and Dad, Vivian Head, Johno Cornish, Judy Soanes, Mark Radcliffe, David Powles, Kevin Creffield, John Hutchinson, Chris Long and Julie Lacey.

ABOUT THE AUTHOR

Alex Boyall lives in Norfolk with wife and youngest son. *Clifton Sands* is his first book.

Contact: alexboyall@yahoo.com

Printed in Great Britain
by Amazon